"In today's rapidly evolving world, leadership requires a nuanced and adaptable approach. *We Are All Ambiverts Now* offers a compelling and insightful exploration of the diverse personality styles that contribute to effective leadership, particularly at the C-suite level. As CEO of the Air France-KLM Group, I've seen firsthand the power of balanced leadership, where individuals can leverage both introverted and extroverted strengths to navigate complex challenges and foster collaboration. This book provides valuable insights for anyone seeking to understand and cultivate the crucial balance needed to succeed in today's dynamic business environment. It's a must-read for current and aspiring leaders alike."

Ben Smith, *CEO Air France-KLM*

"Karl and Gabby have written a book that most senior leaders will find highly instructive. Anyone who chairs several meetings and shakes multiple hands a day, and answers emails in their downtime will be familiar with the dilemmas they outline in their book. I found the insights, gleaned from their interviews with hundreds of senior leaders, highly thought provoking. In an age where the boundary between the 'real world' and the virtual one is getting increasingly blurry, with social media a major consideration for most leaders, striking a balance between introversion and extrovert behaviour is more important than ever. This book is guaranteed to help."

Kamal Munir, *Pro Vice Chancellor at the University of Cambridge, and Professor of Strategy and Policy*

"The authors' thorough and clear depiction of introverts, extroverts, and those in between shine light on the increasing relevance of flexibility and awareness in strong leaders, both in the corporate world and beyond."

Soumitra Dutta, *Peter Moores Dean and Professor of Management, Saïd Business School*

"With grounding in research from Jungian psychology to biochemistry, Maslow to Adam Grant, Kennedy to Clinton—Dr. Moore teaches us that like most things, introversion and extroversion are not black and white but a gradient of color that can add light and dimension to leadership. As versatile as the ambidextrous are with their hands, the ambivert leader is with divergent strengths from listening to allocution. Moore explains that by meeting people where they are, you can get them to go where they need to be. He gives practical guidance to build trust, more productive teams, and the authenticity to excel in an evolving landscape."

Cathy Carlisi *Managing Director, President Emeritus BCG BrightHouse*

"*We Are All Ambiverts Now* by Karl Moore and Gabriele Hartshorne-Mehl is a groundbreaking guide that redefines leadership in today's diverse corporate landscape. Drawing from over 750 interviews with C-suite executives, the authors challenge the traditional belief that leaders must be exclusively extroverted or introverted. Instead, they champion the power of ambiverts—leaders who effortlessly balance both traits.

As a founder and CEO, I've found their strategies instrumental in harmonizing the dynamic between extroverted sales teams and introverted engineering minds, proving that ambiversion is indeed the future of leadership. Chapter 6, 'The Introspective Extrovert,' resonates deeply, highlighting the seamless blend of social prowess and thoughtful introspection essential for effective leadership.

For any leader aiming to build balanced, empowered, and resilient teams, *We Are All Ambiverts Now* is an indispensable resource. It offers a fresh perspective and practical insights that make it essential reading for fostering effective and inclusive leadership".

Daniel Saks, *Co-founder of AppDirect and Landbase, Silicon Valley, USA*

"Every aspiring leader should read this book. As the world changes around us, ambiverts will thrive. This book will give you hope that you can adapt your leadership style, build self-awareness, and succeed."

Asheesh Advani, *CEO, Junior Achievement (JA) Worldwide*

"Everyone can learn something from this book!!"

Daniel Lamarre, *Executive Vice Chairman, Cirque du Soleil Entertainment Group*

"In today's fast-changing world, high quality leadership is more important than ever. In this fascinating book, Karl Moore and Gabriele Hartshorne-Mehl open up the notion of the ambivert leader—someone who is able to adapt to their changing circumstances. The book has fascinating examples of business and political leaders who have mastered the ambivert style, and they offer great advice to all of us, as we seek to become better leaders ourselves."

Julian Birkinshaw, *Dean, Ivey Business School*

"While the world in 2025 remains under the shadow of the VUCA era, Dr. Karl Moore's new book offers a silver lining. As stated in the book, in the face of a turbulent world, leaders must adapt their personality types flexibly and adopt a more inclusive approach.

This idea resonates with the *Yijing*, an ancient Chinese classic. According to the *Yijing*, the nature of the universe lies in the balance of Yin and Yang. Yang represents extroversion—activeness and progressiveness, while Yin represents introversion—cautiousness and thoughtfulness. Successful leadership is best exemplified by the dynamic balance between Yin and Yang. Featuring thought-provoking philosophies and compelling case studies, *We Are All Ambiverts Now* offers valuable insights to businesses and societies worldwide."

Noah Xie, *Chairman of Kmind Consulting*

"Professor Karl Moore's and Gabby's book provides us with vivid, actual examples of why it is beneficial for organizations to nurture diversity. One of the more important benefits of diversity is diversity of thoughts and psychological processing.

As this diversity enables organizations to navigate fast changing environments and achieve superior performance. Introverts and extroverts, and all the various combinations of these two black-and-white conceptualizations, are eloquent examples of this type of diversity."

Quy Huy, *INSEAD Professor of Strategy, The Solvay Chaired Professor of Technological Innovation*

"As a dominant left-hander, my trainer is always working to balance my lopsided strength. The same is equally true for personality types. Moore and Hartshorne-Mehl's decades of extensive research shows how introverted leaders can benefit from *sometimes* acting like more of an extrovert, and that extroverts have much to learn from introverts, too. These insights will help me become a better parent and teacher: I'm not ambivalent about becoming more of an ambivert."

Barry Nalebuff, *Milton Steinbach Professor, Yale School of Management and co-founder, Honest Tea*

"Effective leaders adapt so they can bring their talents and passions to bear on mobilizing people toward their vision of a better tomorrow. Using a wealth of evidence from compelling case studies, Moore and Hartshorne-Mehl demonstrate how to navigate the leadership journey by knowing yourself *and* by learning continually, throughout your life, how to align your values with those of your most important people at work, at home, and in their communities."

Stew Friedman, *Author of* Total Leadership *and Emeritus Professor of Management Practice, The Wharton School, University of Pennsylvania*

"In today's dynamic business landscape, the traditional categories of introverts, ambiverts, and extroverts are evolving, and so must our understanding of leadership. *We Are All Ambiverts Now: Introverts, Ambiverts, and Extroverts in the C-Suite* by Karl Moore and Gabriele Hartshorne-Mehl explores the nuances of personality within the leadership hierarchy, revealing how embracing our diverse traits can foster more innovative, inclusive, and effective leadership. This groundbreaking book encourages aspiring leaders to recognize their strengths, cultivate adaptability, and harness the power of communication and collaboration. Whether you prefer deep thinking or engaging in dynamic brainstorming, it is time to embrace the ambivert within us all and unlock the full potential of diverse leadership styles. The book is a must-read for executives and senior leaders looking to transform their approach to leading, connecting, and thriving in their professional journeys. The book serves as an invaluable, timely, and insightful resource."

Sherif Kamel, *Professor of Management and Dean, Onsi Sawiris School of Business, The American University in Cairo*

"Every once in a while, a book comes out that makes you look at the world, and yourself, a little different. *We Are All Ambiverts Now* is such a book. No more stock assumptions that CEOs are all extroverts or that introverts have to be something they're not to succeed. Like much of leadership, it's not either/or, but both. Such a cool idea, backed by impressive research, that will strip away excuses—imposed or self-imposed—that can keep us sitting on the sidelines when we have every reason to enter the ring."

Sydney Finkelstein *is a professor at Dartmouth's Tuck School of Business and the author of the bestsellers,* Why Smart Executives Fail *and* Superbosses

"This is a splendid read. It features a diverse collection of leaders, all of whom have personally wrestled with the 'vert' matrix during their lives and careers. These leaders have shared their perspectives as part of Moore's research for this Work, which enables readers to expand their own understanding of how effective leadership can be exercised. My review brought to mind two excerpts from the works of William Shakespeare that focus on the phenomenon of role-playing and how personal values remain a foundational element of genuine leadership. The first is from *As You Like It*:

All the world's a stage,
And all the men and women merely players.
They have their exits and their entrances;
And one man in his time plays many parts.

The second is from *Hamlet*, as part of the advice given by Polonius to his son Laertes:

This above all: to thine own self be true.
And it must follow, as the night the day,
Thou canst not then be false to any man.

On occasion, leaders must be prepared to act, seemingly out of character (even in roles with which they may be uncomfortable), but while harnessing those role-playing tactics, never compromise their values."

Richard Pound, *Olympic Athlete and Olympic Committee (IOC) Member for over 40 years*

We Are All Ambiverts Now

Based on real-world evidence from senior executives and successful entrepreneurs, this book argues that an effective leader must act like an ambivert: an introvert at times and an extrovert at others.

Thanks to landmark books such as *How to Win Friends and Influence People*, many professionals think that only extroverts can be standout leaders, but Karl Moore's interviews with over 750 CEOs from around the world prove that introverts make excellent leaders too. These insights make clear that the optimal leadership style is ambivert, with senior leaders combining introversion—being excellent listeners and thinking before they speak—and extroversion—inspiring and connecting with their teams. This book teaches how introverts and extroverts work, manage, and lead effectively and how readers can be better leaders regardless of their natural communication style. It empowers leaders to celebrate the strengths of their personality type while being flexible and to understand when to incorporate the strengths of other types into their leadership approach to be more effective. While showing how to identify and utilize the approach that is best for a given situation, it also highlights the potential weaknesses of the ambivert's chameleon nature and emphasizes the importance of leaders staying true to themselves in any situation.

Current and aspiring leaders, as well as entrepreneurs and MBA and executive education students, will understand how to develop and maximize the perfect blend of introversion and extroversion as this book guides them through a range of potential situations encountered in the workplace.

Karl Moore is Associate Professor in the Desautels Faculty of Management at McGill University and an Associate of Green Templeton College, Oxford University. He hosts a weekly Canadian national radio programme, "The CEO Series," an hour-long one-on-one with CEOs, and is a regular contributor to *Forbes.com*.

Gabriele Hartshorne-Mehl graduated with Distinction from McGill University's Desautels Faculty of Management, completing a degree in Finance and Political Science, and is a JD Candidate at Osgoode Hall Law School, York University, where she also serves as Senior Editor of the *Osgoode Hall Law Journal*.

We Are All Ambiverts Now

Introverts, Ambiverts, and Extroverts in the C-Suite

Karl Moore and
Gabriele Hartshorne-Mehl

Routledge
Taylor & Francis Group

NEW YORK AND LONDON

Designed cover image: David Drummond

First published 2026
by Routledge
605 Third Avenue, New York, NY 10158

and by Routledge
4 Park Square, Milton Park, Abingdon, Oxon, OX14 4RN

Routledge is an imprint of the Taylor & Francis Group, an informa business

ISBN: 978-1-041-00911-5 (hbk)
ISBN: 978-1-041-00910-8 (pbk)
ISBN: 978-1-003-61221-6 (ebk)

DOI: 10.4324/9781003612216

Typeset in Times New Roman
by Apex CoVantage, LLC

Contents

For my wife Brigitte and our children, Erik and Marie-Eve!

- Karl

Thank you to my Mom and Dad, for always supporting me.

- Gabriele

Introduction

A Paradigm Shift in the Way We Think About Introverts and Extroverts

An important topic in leadership today is that of the introverted leader. Susan Cain's *New York Times* bestseller *Quiet*[1] sheds light on the important yet overlooked effects of introversion on daily interactions, relationships, and major life decisions. It also stimulated considerable interest in the idea that introverts can provide tremendous value in a world where extroverts tend to be more dominant. Cain's movement in support of introverted leadership has encouraged the appreciation of quiet leaders everywhere as mainstream leadership continues to diversify its traditional preference towards extroverts in charge. Prior to discussing this matter in detail—which will come later—we would like to share how our interest in the topic came about—our origin story, if you will.

Back in 2010, Emma Bambrick (at the time, an undergrad student of Karl's who now works as a partner for management consultant Carpedia International) and Karl wrote a review of Susan Cain's book for Karl's regular piece for *Forbes.com*. This article received 500 times more attention than the vast majority of his other weekly column contributions for *Forbes*. Clearly, this was a topic that resonated with people—and a lot of them. Looking back, such great interest should not have surprised us: everyone in the world, regardless of gender, or race, or nationality, etc. falls somewhere on the introvert-extrovert continuum.

The following Wednesday evening, Karl had his weekly MBA CEO Insights class. Every week, two or three CEOs are invited into the class for an hour each. On this particular evening, the first guest was Claude Mongeau, then the CEO of Canadian National Railroad, which had approximately 24,000 employees—a big organization by any standard. Karl asked Claude a question he had never asked anyone before: "Are you more of an introvert or extrovert?"

Claude went on for about ten minutes in a quiet way about being very introverted. He shared the story that when he was COO, CN's number two, the board told him they were considering making him CEO, but that he needed to act less shy and more assertive—in their actual words, he had to be more extroverted. One board member suggested they hire Claude a leadership coach. This coach told Claude that five times a day he had to act like an extrovert. He gave Claude a

DOI: 10.4324/9781003612216-1

clicker, similar to one a bouncer uses to keep count of people in a bar. Five times a day, Claude had to act like an extrovert and click the clicker.

One example of "extroverted behaviour" he gave was as follows: when getting in the elevator in the morning, rather than looking at his feet and thinking about how to save CN money, he needed to say hello to others by name, comment on the weather, and thank them for their recent presentation. That is what chief executives do, his coach told him; the clicker helped him learn that side of leadership. He would report back to his coach routinely to measure his extroverted growth. Claude's story shows that extroverted behaviour can be learned and encouraged in a positive manner among the people who work for you. It is a good leader-like, CEO-like behaviour.

The second CEO invited to the class was an introvert as well. Frankly, Karl was rather surprised.

Susan Cain, in *Quiet*, produced a conclusion of great interest to us:

> Our lives are shaped as profoundly by personality as by gender or race. And the single most important aspect of personality—the 'north and south of temperament,' as one scientist puts it—is where we fall on the introvert-extrovert spectrum. Our place on this continuum influences our choice of friends and mates, and how we make conversation, resolve differences, and show love. It affects the careers we choose and whether or not we succeed at them. It governs how likely we are to . . . be a good leader.[1]

The main idea explored in this book is that almost all the hundreds of executives Karl has spoken with reported that they frequently must adapt their personality type depending on what's required of them in a particular situation. Put simply, his interviews have led him to the conclusion that in order to be successful, it is essential for business leaders to act on a regular basis, like the other personality types. Those who are more introverted need to act a bit more extroverted on occasion, and those who are more extroverted need to pull back in certain instances. That is, in short, act like an ambivert. An ambivert is perhaps a new term for many readers. It was invented in the 20s and has almost entirely dropped from the physiology and management literature and hence our thinking. We would like to bring this term back to life.

Another big trend in corporations and elsewhere is EDI: Equity, Diversity, and Inclusion. Karl, as an older person, has worked to add age to the conversation, and he also suggested that social class is important, having grown up in a lower-middle-class income family. Undoubtedly, race and gender are the most important and the ones that people are most apt to run into discrimination on a regular basis in the workplace. We believe personality type, as an additional dimension of diversity between individuals, should be added to the list of things to consider under the scope of EDI. That the negative bias against introverts has decreased in comparison to the workplace of twenty years ago or even a decade ago is laudable—but we believe there is still too little recognition of the considerable strengths of introverts.

A central purpose of this book is to present evidence that we hope will shift readers' perceptions of introverts as leaders in an even more positive direction. Beyond that, we aim to encourage senior leaders and people who wish to be more senior leaders to learn to act like an extrovert at times and an introvert at other times—that is, to approach leadership and communication with balance and flexibility, despite any natural dispositions to lean too far one way.

We believe that introverts and extroverts alike possess qualities that can contribute to a leader's effectiveness. However, we want to suggest another idea: why must good leaders be one or the other? We wish to highlight the idea of ambiverts as a personality type senior leaders should strive to model, all while staying true to their authentic selves. Our authentic self is somewhere on the bell curve from very extroverted at one end and very introverted at the other end, though the considerable majority of people are not at the ends of the curve.

One of Karl's undergraduate students in 2024 was Brielle Robillard. Brielle, though only 21, has been a working actor for over a decade, known for various Hollywood films (Place of Bones, The Silencing) and TV shows. Karl discussed the idea that you have to "act" like the other, and it resonated with her. Here are her comments:

When building a character, I find that extroversion and introversion are foundational. Extroverted characters often have a vivid outer life; they're performers, connectors, and natural communicators. On the other hand, I learn about introverted characters by deepening their inner worlds—allowing them space to be listeners, thinkers, and creators. As an actor, tuning into both worlds within myself is essential to fully embody each role. This is applicable to the working world at large. If you can build an inner and outer life within your own identity, you can be a skilled and adaptable ambivert. If you're introverted, think of facets of your life that challenge you to express yourself outwardly, and if you're extroverted, challenge yourself to embrace pieces of your identity that are more independent of others' influences. Practice this exercise in comfortable settings and then apply it to parts of your life where it is necessary. Personally, I feel this interplay as I shift between acting and writing. In acting, I lean on my extroverted side, engaging outwardly with others' emotions and reactions. In writing, I become more introverted, fully immersed in my inner creative world. This duality served me well as a student in Professor Moore's class; in discussions, I was able to communicate actively but then relied on my introversion to internalize knowledge with humility.

We're always building both our inner and outer identities, often without realizing it. But when we approach this process as if we're getting to know a new character, we can make it conscious and productive.

A friend of Karl's, this one in her 50s, is a TV host and world-class photographer; here are Heidi Hollinger's thoughts:

> I am an ambivert for optimal flow. I draw energy from social interactions and from time alone which I prize. My mother is Finnish which makes me inclined to appreciate personal space, privacy and silence. Having said that, I am naturally gregarious, I love talking to everyone and anyone I meet in the street, pretty much always striking up conversations as soon as I exit my house. I got that from my dad. We would have lunch in a diner, and it seemed like he spoke with everyone but me! He loved to make people laugh and remembered every single joke he ever heard. Just before he died, he said to me, 'Heidi, you love people.' And I do.
>
> That is why I feel so especially at home in Cuba where the people are incredibly friendly, outgoing and kind. My mom finds it so exasperating when she visits me in Havana, as everyone, even complete strangers are kissing her hello (lucky for her it's just one cheek unlike two in Québec!).
>
> In my career as a photographer and TV host, it served me well to be an extrovert. In studio sessions, I would speak with my subjects, putting them at ease and distracting them until they were unguarded and authentic to capture, as Henri Cartier-Bresson would say, 'the decisive moment' when all elements in the scene were aligned. During the filming of my TV show Waterfront Cities of the World, I would need to be outgoing and open to keep the conversations with my guests engaging and lively. While writing my books on Russia and Cuba, I needed to align with my inner introvert to channel my focus into writing, which demanded a lot from me!
>
> At this point in particular in my life, in my 50's, I am choosing to be more introspective, mindful and therefore more introverted. I've reached the phase that Carl Yung would refer to as the Statement, a time to reflect on what one has accomplished, and how to continue moving forward.

We will come back to Brielle's comments on acting when we discuss in more detail how senior leaders must learn to act like the other personality type in order to be more effective senior leaders. And Heidi's about introversion/extroversion in different cultures (she mentions Finnish and Cuban), and in her role as a tv show host.

The Research Underlying This Book

Karl spent 11 years with IBM and Hitachi before his academic career. He recalled very clearly how in the 80s and 90s individuals were taught by senior leaders, through example, if not explicitly, a model of a purely extroverted approach to leadership. Some years ago, when Karl first looked at the leadership literature that mentioned personality, it was almost universally suggested that the considerable majority of senior leaders were extroverts. When we delved into the literature, however, very few researchers had actually talked to senior leaders. Most references to executive management involved books/articles written by former CEOs that primarily reflected on their lives or careers—they were one person's story. These sources typically did not deal directly with the question of personality type.

Most of the research about introverts and extroverts is published by psychology professors, whose subjects are largely undergraduates. Professors have an endless supply of undergraduates whom they can, as a legitimate part of their classes, instruct to take personality tests. Undergraduates are great for statistics, but they do not provide insight into the experiences of executives seasoned in the corporate world. While the research that Karl read was insightful, there were very few, if any, studies done concerning the C-suite. Executive management in the C-suite is typically in their 40s or older, so they have grown and evolved as leaders. They are quite different people than they were during their undergraduate degrees.

Over the past decade, Karl has been filling this gap by interviewing over 750 CEOs and other C-suite executives. C-suite executives are senior leaders whose title begins with "C", CEO but also Chief Operating Officer (COO), Chief Financial Officer (CFO), Chief Marketing Officer (CMO), Chief Information Office (CIO), Chief Technology Officer (CTO), Chief Digital Officer (CDO), Chief Human Resources Officer (CHRO) and EIEIO (Old McDonald had a farm—an attempt at humour!). The findings that he has gathered from these interviews lie at the core of this book.

Beyond the CEO Insights MBA course and his research on this subject, for about a decade, Karl has hosted a weekly national radio show, the CEO Series, an hour-long one-on-one with various CEOs heard across Canada on the Bell Media network. You can hear it as a podcast on *Apple, iHeart, Spotify*, etc.

One advantage of age is that as you get older, quite a bit older, like Karl, you have done something for a long time. Karl started interviewing CEOs for his PhD back in the early 1990s. In the 1980s, he worked for IBM, where he participated in IBM's "CEO sell." Computers, known then as Black Box mainframes, were a considerable mystery to most executives. These senior officials understood Black Boxes were important, but the concept was novel (rather like AI today). IBM salespeople marketed computers to the CEO as a way of moving their organization successfully towards the future of business. Karl learned that his successful sales experiences would often involve younger, junior employees of the CEO teaming up with Karl to demonstrate the convenience of modern technology and convince the CEO that Black Boxes were a worthy upgrade. This observation formed the basis of Karl's future research interests, both as a PhD student and later, as a professor.

Karl earned his PhD at York University Schulich School of Business and the University of Toronto's Rotman School of Business. He interviewed CEOs for his research, where he analyzed Canadian subsidiaries of US global multinationals and how they earned global responsibilities. For example, IBM Canada made products that were sold around the world. These global products mainly came from IBM's home country of the US, but led other subsidiaries, like Canada, Germany, the UK, etc., would also be capable of developing, managing and helping other subsidiaries sell these global products. The CEO of the Canadian subsidiary was a central actor in earning these global responsibilities and retaining them over time. Having learned the CEO sell at IBM, Karl interviewed a considerable number of CEOs for his thesis, it was perhaps not a surprise that his CEO Series radio show, CEO Insights MBA class, was a somewhat natural outgrowth of this earlier work. The net result is that Karl has interviewed over 1,000 CEOs, among the most around the world for professors at Business Schools, but on the other hand, it has taken over 30 years to hit this number (Karl would rather be younger and have hair, but c'est la vie)!

Gabriele has been the producer of the CEO Series for almost two years and several times has done a producer's cut on the interview, providing Gen Z's thoughts on the CEOs' comments. Many of the interviews Karl has done on the show are cited in this book. In the conversations for the show, he covers a few subjects and asks his guests a wide variety of questions, such as: how do you handle mental stress since the pandemic? How do you help your staff handle mental stress? What are you doing about AI? How are you dealing with Gen Z? How do you do strategy in the real world? And what is your purpose? Most crucially, however, for several years, Karl has been asking each of them about being an introvert or extrovert and how that impacts their leadership.

This book is focused largely on leaders in the C-suite who are typically more apt to be the age of the parents of undergraduates instead of undergraduates themselves. Many of these people are 20 or more years deep into their careers and have developed a great deal since their college days in their early twenties. Not only do they have decades more of life experience, but they are also among the top ranks of leaders in their organization. Time after time, these executives have been viewed by their managers as exceptional leaders. They have made it to the top of their respective organizations, whether that be running Fortune 500 Companies, an NGO, or a ministry in a government.

Of course, Karl has also included in the scope of his research an emphasis on young entrepreneurs and startup founders, many of whom used to attend his CEO Insights class as MBA students of McGill. Although younger than those senior leaders of the C-suite, these successful individuals are also considerably experienced and offer equally beneficial insight into corporate success. Ten or fifteen years ago, the dream careers for many BComs (business undergraduates) were a position at MBB (McKinsey, Bain or Boston Consulting Group—the top three management consultant firms) or working as an investment banker. Although those two are undeniably still popular today, being an entrepreneur is a third type of career that has emerged as equally prestigious to many BComs. The world moves on.

This book will draw much on academic research, both from existing literature as well as the interview-based research Karl and his team have done over the last thirteen years. It will focus on introverts, extroverts, and ambiverts as leaders. Karl's team comprises a few dozen undergraduate and MBA students from McGill University and Oxford University, where Karl worked as a faculty member full-time for five years and part-time for the last 20 or so years. Along the way, Karl has had the opportunity to work with Susan Cain and her Quiet Leadership Institute. Twice, Karl visited and worked at Quiet House, where the Institute is housed just outside of New York City, interviewed her for the CEO Series radio show, Canada's *National Post* newspaper, etc. and wrote with her and others for the Quiet Leadership Institute.

The main insights that he has gathered further challenge the once-rampant and still prominent view that executives must be extroverted. In reality, many interviewees identified as strong introverts.

Putting Outdated Ideas Away

One of the more fascinating people Karl has interviewed was General Martin Dempsey, a four-star general who was the Chairman of the Joint Chiefs of Staff under President Obama. Karl taught with him on an executive programme at Duke University, where the General had completed a master's in literature earlier in life. The Chairman of the Joint Chiefs is the most senior general in the US, by extension, one of the most senior generals in the world. He shared with Karl an old saying in the military, that "generals fight the battles of their youth." The point he was making was that you learn much about leadership and strategy in your twenties in the military.

He gave the example of how he was a pup lieutenant out of West Point and had his first command during the Cold War in Germany. He learned leadership and strategy from that experience in his 20s and from watching and being mentored by the majors and colonels who had learned strategy and leadership in the Vietnam War. Martin became a general and served as a commander in Iraq. He said that because of rapidly changing times, the valuable lessons of strategy and leadership he had gathered from the Vietnam vets from his time in the Cold War were much less applicable to Iraq and, later, to his position as chairman.

How do you not become yesterday's person? As Karl is now in his 60s, this is a pressing concern, whereas Gabriele, in her early 20s, has much less, if almost anything, to unlearn. The view that only extroverts are leaders is one of those critical leadership lessons that we must unlearn and toss over the side of the boat. It is dated, inaccurate, and it gets in the way of doing our best in today's world.

What is more interesting and what will be one of the main ideas explored in this book, is that almost all of the executives Karl has spoken with reported that they frequently have to adapt their personality type to some degree depending on what's required of them in a particular situation. Put simply, his interviews have led him to the conclusion that in order to be successful, it is essential for business leaders to act, on a regular basis, like the other personality types. Those who are more introverted need to act a bit more extroverted on occasion, and those who are more extroverted need to pull back in certain instances.

We want to introduce a new term to describe versatile leaders with both sets of qualities: ambiverts. Ambiverts are individuals who can behave both like an introvert and like an extrovert, depending on what the situation calls for. Throughout the following chapters, we will argue the merits of being an ambiverted leader and how, in today's world, successful leaders are those who can be both great listeners like introverts but also sociable and decisive like extroverts.

Based on prior literature, the leadership community had assumed that senior leaders were largely extroverts. In the interviews we have done for this book, we have concluded that among senior leaders, in business but also in NGOs, government and even the military, about 40% are introverts, 40% are extroverts, and about 20% are genuine ambiverts.

Introversion and extroversion follow a bell curve: there are people like Karl who lie more towards the extremes (extrovert in his case), but most people are just a bit introverted or extroverted (like Gabriele, who is slightly extroverted but much more so in the middle than Karl). When Karl first came across the term ambivert and was dealing with three categories, not two, he had assumed that it would be an even split. Our research suggests, however, that a smaller number are true ambiverts.

We hope to provide the reader with an expanded view of what introverts, extroverts, and ambiverts can all bring to the table as C-suite executives. We will endeavour to paint a clear picture of the strengths and weaknesses of each group, and we will draw on our interviews to highlight key examples of how different business executives (and some prime ministers, cabinet ministers, generals and senior politicians) have managed to overcome their naturally predisposed weaknesses, while at the same time playing to their strengths.

Karl finds that as a very extroverted person himself, it can be exhausting for him to act like an introvert, but it is a necessary discipline which enables Karl to be a better leader, husband and father. We hope to teach readers strategies for adopting this flexibility all while remaining authentic. After all, one of the most important traits of a leader today is to be authentic, to be real, to be themselves.

We believe the ideas in this book go beyond the workplace. In our minds, it suggests a better understanding of personality dynamics in today's world.

As this book will argue, the idea of having a degree of fluidity between introversion and extroversion is not just a skill for top executives but a vital tool for anyone navigating the challenges of life. By understanding the strengths and challenges of our own personality and learning to blend introvert and extrovert qualities at the appropriate times, we can handle different situations in life better. Whether it's in our friendships, community activities, or jobs, having this balance helps us respond more effectively. This book is an invitation to explore the ambivert in each of us, seeking new possibilities for success in every aspect of our lives.

Note

1 Cain, S. *Quiet: The Power of Introverts in a World that Can't Stop Talking*, 74. Crown Publishing Group, 2012.

Chapter 1

The Strengths of Extroverted Leaders and Where They Fall Short

For many years, the top leaders of the Western world were seen largely to be extroverts and extroverts alone. Their energy and charisma have proven an asset for leadership throughout history and across industries. This assumption is not entirely inappropriate: prominent leaders like Bill Clinton, Margaret Thatcher, George W. Bush, Muhammad Ali, Boris Yeltsin, Winston Churchill, Brian Mulroney, John Turner, etc., suggest that extroverted personalities often dominate the leadership landscape. Beyond politics, business executives like Richard Branson, Mark Cuban, and Steve Jobs are all leaders that scholars such as Nobel, Mueller, and Cain have pointed to as clearly extroverted leaders.[1]

We asked two longtime astute journalists, who had covered the US presidents and Canadian prime ministers since the 1960s, how some of North America's leaders might fall on the continuum of more introverted or extroverted. One of these journalists was David Shribman, a Pulitzer Prize winner who worked at the *Wall Street Journal* and the *New York Times* as their Washington bureau chief and later became the Editor in Chief of the *Pittsburgh Post-Gazette*. Today, he is a columnist for Canada's *Globe and Mail* and teaches at McGill University in Montréal. As the Washington bureau chief, he spent thousands of hours over many years observing the US presidents. In short, he is an American journalist who has known many of the US presidents in our lifetime and has also been a keen observer of the Canadian prime ministers as well.

The other journalist was Lisa Van Dusen, a *Policy Magazine* editor, publisher and political columnist. Formerly an international writer for Peter Jennings at ABC News, editor at UPI Washington and AP National New York, director of media relations for McGill University, Washington columnist for the *Ottawa Citizen* and Sun Media, senior writer for *Maclean*'s, and press assistant to Prime Minister Brian Mulroney. In short, a Canadian who knows US and Canadian politicians very well.

What surprised Karl, who remembers these political figures from his childhood in the 1960s and has hosted six of the Prime Ministers (Clark, Mulroney, Chretien, Martin, Harper, and Trudeau) in his CEO Class for MBAs or on his radio show and thus has had the chance to discuss their introversion/extroversion

DOI: 10.4324/9781003612216-2

with them, was how many identified as introverts. Karl's surprise came largely from the fact that these figures all had to be retail politicians for at least part of the time and, as the leader of the country, were the centre of attention in almost every context they found themselves in—you would think, as Karl did, that this position would demand an extrovert. Table 1.1 shows their responses when asked about their personality type or David and Lisa's thoughts.

Extroverts indeed possess strengths of considerable value for senior executives and anyone hoping to climb the corporate ladder—our system was, at least in the past, built for them to a considerable degree. Nowadays, we are more open to more introverted leaders such as President Obama, Richard Nixon, Hillary

Table 1.1 Introversion and Extroversion of Presidents and Prime Ministers Since the 1960s

Name	Introvert	Extrovert	Comments if any
US Presidents			
John F. Kennedy	x	x	Ambivert
Lyndon B. Johnson		x	
Richard M. Nixon	x		
Jimmy Carter	x		
Ronald Reagan		x	
George H.W. Bush		x	
William Clinton	x	x	Ambivert
George W. Bush		x	
Barack Obama	x		
Donald Trump		x	
Joe Biden		x	
Canadian Prime Ministers			
Lester, Pearson	x		
Pierre Trudeau	x	x	Ambivert
Joe Clark	x		
John Turner		x	
Brian Mulroney		x	
Kim Campbell	x		
Jean Chretien		x	
Paul Martin	x		
Stephen Harper	x		
Justin Trudeau	x	x	Ambivert

Clinton, Bill Gates, Warren Buffett, Elon Musk, Marissa Mayer, and many, many more.[2]

Warren Buffett—The World's Richest Introvert?

Twice, in 2006 and 2017, Karl took students from McGill to spend a day with Warren Buffett in Omaha, and one time had lunch with Mr. Buffett and a few students. There is no question that he is an introvert based on our discussion. May 5, 2017, Karl wrote a *Forbes.com* piece on the visits, "Two days with Warren Buffett: three lessons from an introverted leader in action."[3] What follows is some of what he wrote:

> Warren Buffett is one of the world's greatest businesspeople and well-known as an introvert, so it was fascinating to spend the better part of a day with him and about 100 college students recently in Omaha. Just over 10 years ago, in 2006, I took 40 McGill University students for a similar visit with Mr. Buffett at his offices in Omaha and then had lunch as his guests at his favorite Omaha restaurant. This time, I was there with my introverted leadership researcher hat firmly on. Over the last three years, I have interviewed over 250 executives about introverts in the C-suite, mainly CEOs. I have also shadowed some of these executives in order to watch them in action, leading as quiet, or introverted, leaders. So when this opportunity arose, I was excited to watch one of the world's greatest investors, business leaders and best known introverts in action.
>
> We used to wonder whether introverts could make excellent executives. That idea is clearly on its way out. Warren Buffett is a great business leader whose words and actions are watched with interest by millions worldwide. Many, many of my students applied to spend the time with him.
>
> Three things stood out to me as I watched him in action doing his Q&A with us, at lunch, in taking group pictures and chatting with us. Reflecting back to a decade ago, these three things were clearly also in evidence then. They are a part of what an introvert is. Firstly, Mr. Buffett spoke easily, comfortably and with very considerable authority, but only about things that he knew about—that, as an 87-year-old, he had worked on, thought about and studied for decades in most cases. Our research suggests that this is very typical of introverted leaders. Extroverts, like myself, are too apt to make it up as we go along; this, of course, can get us into trouble, as it should. Introverts can be just as good communicators as extroverts, but almost always stick to things they know. Mr. Buffett did not pontificate on things that were outside of his expertise, which at his age and experience is a pretty broad set of subjects.
>
> Another thing that struck me was how his answers were almost gem-like in their well thought phrasing and wordsmithing. The students had clearly done

their homework, having read books about his life and poured over interviews done with him. What made Warren so believable was his having answered the same, or at least similar, questions before and having beautiful, almost gem-like answers. In our research, introverts are often people who fuss over words and wrestle with phrases so that when they do discuss something, they are very well prepared and have mentally edited their answers so they are very, very good. I have written a few times with my more introverted colleague Henry Mintzberg. Besides being very smart and having studied management since the 1960s, part of the secret to Henry's success as a management scholar and writer is how he edits, and edits, and edits. He works on the phrasing so much that his writing is simply better than most other management thinkers. At first it was a bit frustrating, particularly as an extrovert, but the fruits of this tedious labour have convinced me to be more like Henry and Warren when I write. No wonder both have so many memorable quotes and sayings—they take the time to craft them.

The third and final note was that Warren did his networking as an introvert often does, in small numbers and not worrying about working the crowd as much as an extrovert would. He very graciously took a group picture with each school, but at lunch he sat virtually the whole time with six students and talked to them one or two at a time. He had a real conversation with them and did not flit from one table to another as I do when I am giving a talk with a similar number of people. In fact, I gave a talk on my research on introvert/ambivert/extrovert leaders to a similar number of people in Iceland, where I hardly know a soul. I worked the room and connected with every table. But having watched Mr. Buffett the week before, I decided I needed to be a better leader and act like him and have some real in-depth conversation rather than just briefly connect with people. Yet another lesson learned from this great man.

Introverted leaders tell me that they have to act like an extrovert in some contexts to be the leader that the moment requires. Watching Mr. Buffett in action reinforced for me that what is good for the goose is good for the gander, and that for me to be a better leader, at times, I need to act like an introvert and do the three things that I saw Mr. Buffett do. Speak about what you know well, work on expressing ideas very clearly and take time to have real, in-depth conversations with people.

In the more distant past, we had tended to perceive extroverts as better business leaders, as their social skills, confidence, and decisiveness were seemingly more compatible with the surface-level job description of the average executive.[4] Their success was frequently attributed to their extroverted traits, which seemed, at times, to align more naturally with leadership roles. However, the old-school view of labelling extroversion as a straightforward ticket to leadership success is, we argue, seriously inaccurate in today's world. While it's true that extroverted qualities can be advantageous in some situations, truly understanding what it means to be an extrovert requires digging deeper. We argue that introverts can, at times, demonstrate the more positive aspects of these traits in a helpful and authentic way and bring real strengths that extroverts should seek to learn as well—a two-way street.[5]

We will begin by exploring the strengths and challenges of an extroverted personality and diving into how these traits impact both their professional and personal lives. This chapter aims to establish a strong understanding of the alluring, sometimes rambunctious, irritatingly noisy, and "centre of attention" extroverts. It will explore the systems in which they thrive, their strengths and shortcomings, and their potential opportunities for growth. We believe this will be of interest to both extroverts (it is all about you, after all) but also to introverts who work with, lead, are led by, and have family members who are extroverts. In our experience, if introverts can better understand and perhaps sympathize with extroverts, they can work more effectively with them.

Extroverts are differentiated from their quieter, more introspective coun-terparts through their seeking stimulation and a more outward/external orien-tation. General characteristics of this archetype include friendliness, humour, light-heartedness, the ability to improvise, positivity, confidence, impulsiveness, outspokenness, and sometimes being domineering.[6]

Carl Jung

Let's go back to the beginning. The great pioneering Swiss psychoanalyst and psychiatrist Carl Jung first introduced the terms *introvert* and *extrovert* in his book *Psychological Types*, published in 1921 and translated from German to English in 1923, bringing them to the field of psychology and a worldwide audi-ence. Although terms have evolved since then, his definitions remain relevant today and add some depth and colour beyond the central idea of seeking stimu-lation. According to Jung, the extrovert's "whole consciousness looks outward, because the essential and decisive determination always comes from outside."[7] He believes that the extrovert has an objective attitude because he "allows him-self to be oriented by the given facts."[8] Thus,

> if a man thinks, feels, acts, and actually lives in a way that is directly corre-lated with the objective conditions and their demands, he is extroverted. His life makes it perfectly clear that it is the object and not this subjective view that plays the determining role in his consciousness.[9]

Extroverts are primarily concerned with the context in which they find them-selves. Not inclined to take a subjective view of the situation, they have a reactive attitude that enables them to act directly in the event of a crisis. They will look for answers outside, in the world, by talking to managers and coming up with an immediate plan of action to solve the problems they perceive. This move to action is a central part of many extroverts' lives.

As an extrovert on the far end of the bell curve, Karl tends to make quick decisions, such as when ordering in a restaurant (and gets impatient with those who give it much thought).

Extroversion has its benefits. Karl recalls being with a student group in the Singapore airport about a decade ago, flying back from eight days in Indonesia. In the Singapore airport, there were hundreds of people on their way to and from flights. There was an escalator in the middle of the terminal that had been stopped, and two men were helping a man who was lying down at the top of the escalator, evidently in pain. Without thought, Karl called out in a loud voice, "Is there a doctor in the house?" A moment later, a man carrying a medical bag came running. Karl simply pointed at the three men on the escalator, and, much like a football tight end, the man made a beeline to and ran up the escalator. It was a moment of high drama that hundreds watched, and then they turned towards Karl, and they started applauding. He turned to the undergraduate beside him and said, "Everyone over 30 is kicking themselves and asking why they didn't do that?" It was an obvious thing, in retrospect, to do. That is one of those occasions where action without thought pays off. Karl could also share hundreds of times that it got him in trouble! More on that later.

Jung described extroverts as actively engaged with their surroundings: they are attracted to and develop relationships with objects in their social environment; they are quick to adjust to this environment as it changes; and they perceive circumstances around them quickly (albeit imperfectly).[10] The extrovert undertakes energy interactions in their environment for deliberation or decision-making, idea brainstorming, and thought processing. In their purest form, they draw energy from their surroundings and release similar energy back into their environment—a positive feedback loop that might look like a buildup of lively social chatter and magnetism, if you will.

> On the other hand, his normality must also depend essentially on whether he takes account of his subjective needs and requirements, and this is just his weak point, for the tendency of his type is so outer directed that even the most obvious of all subjective facts, the condition of his own body, receives scant attention.[11]

Chemical Differences Between Extroverts and Introverts

In her book *The Introvert Advantage*, Dr. Laney's research finds chemical differences in the brains of introverts and extroverts that suggest the validity of

Jung's work.[12] Laney cites a study conducted by Dr. Johnson and published in the *American Journal of Psychiatry*: through PET scans of introverts and extroverts, Johnson determines that blood flow for each group occurs along different pathways in the brain.[13] Extroverted blood flows through areas where visual, auditory, tactile, and taste sensory processing occurs, whereas introverted blood flows through sectors more involved with internal experiences like memory and problem-solving. From this finding, we may infer that behavioural differences between introverts and extroverts are related to their use of different pathways that influence whether the focus is directed internally or externally.

The primary blood pathway in the brains of extroverts, which is shorter and less internally focused, requires dopamine to regulate it. Laney argues that extroverts are less sensitive to dopamine, thus are more apt to seek it out and may be categorized as high-novelty seekers. She cites a study on high-novelty seekers by Hamer of the National Cancer Institute. This demographic requires thrilling experiences and consistent change to produce adequate dopamine levels in their system. They also dislike routine and repetitive work. High-novelty seekers tend to pursue dopamine's effects more often than low-novelty-seeking introverts in their external environment through new and exciting situations. Introverts, on the other hand, are more likely to feel overstimulated by such interactions.[14] This conclusion is consistent with Jung's hypothesis that extroverts are attracted to their unpredictable and dynamic external environment.

The sympathetic nervous system increases the dilation of pupils, speeds up the pumping of blood by the heart, constricts blood vessels to prevent injury, and slows down digestion processes to prepare for faster decision-making. This system is activated during situations perceived as emergencies by the brain. It is also the primary system available to humans in their first two years of life, as it provides the capacity to explore the world around us. In another scenario, the sympathetic system attracts us to new experiences. As we employ it, the system releases energy by sending dopamine transmitters to our brains. As extroverts prefer dopamine pathways, they also tend to use their sympathetic nervous system more often than introverts.[15] Extroverts are naturally attuned to external stimuli and social interactions. Their neural pathways, primarily governed by dopamine, crave novelty and dynamic experiences.

Alcohol, Finances, and Extroverts

How might our personality type mould our alcohol consumption? Research reveals that individuals with more pronounced extroverted traits tend to experiment with alcohol at a younger age and exhibit a propensity for heavier drinking in non-clinical groups compared to their introverted counterparts.[16] What underpins this personality-based divergence in drinking behaviours?

Surprisingly, past research has shown that the mood-lifting effects of alcohol do not significantly differ between extroverts and introverts. However, these previous studies looked at alcohol consumption in isolation; looking at group interactions paints a different picture. In a group drinking paradigm, individuals high in extraversion gained greater rewards from alcohol than those low in extraversion. The mood-enhancing effect of alcohol on extroverts was explained by their tendency to associate greater reward with the genuine smiles and other outward behaviour displayed by their fellow group mates, an insight aligned with Jung's definition of extroverts as actively engaged with their surroundings.[17]

Another study reveals the relationship between extroversion and household finances. Brown and Taylor (2013) explore the relationship between personality and levels of debt and assets held.[18] Interestingly, for extroverts, this relationship bears a correlation that is often relatively large. Their study reveals that, out of the Big Five Personality Traits (Openness to experience, Conscientiousness, Extraversion, Agreeableness, and Neuroticism), extroverted individuals have the largest statistical association with debt in magnitude. In other words, the more extroverted you are, the more unsecured debt you are expected to accumulate. This finding suggests extroverts are more prone to taking risks and is further consistent with Jung's views.

The Big Five Versus the Myers-Briggs

By and large, the research community tends to see the Big Five as more scientifically valid than the very widely used Myers-Briggs test. However, the Myers-Briggs test is highly regarded in business. The test has four key dimensions: 1. Introvert versus Extrovert, 2. Sensing versus Intuitive, 3. Thinking versus Feeling, 4. Perceiving versus Judging. The Myers-Briggs system identifies clear preferences, allowing you to be categorized according to an "either/or" format. In contrast, the Big Five personality model uses a continuum, providing a percentage for each of the five personality traits. Thus, it is argued, we think with considerable justification, that some degree of nuance is built directly into the Big Five system. This is often regarded as one reason why personality researchers have a higher level of trust in their results. An article in *Scientific American* in the February 28, 2024, issue reported on a study based on 559 respondents and found on average, the Big Five test was about twice as accurate as the MBTI-style test for predicting these life outcomes, not perfect for sure, but not bad.[19] The authors concluded that, on average, the Big Five test was about twice as accurate as the MBTI-style test for predicting these life outcomes. So, we have focused on research and work on the Big Five.

But to give the Myers-Briggs company its due credit, it is very widely used. Merve Emre, an English professor at the University of Oxford (formerly at McGill) and herself a former consultant for the firm Bain & Co., thoroughly covered the rise of the indicator in her 2018 book.[20] The questionnaire's history begins with the mother-daughter duo Katharine Cook Briggs and Isabel Briggs Myers. Katharine graduated from Michigan Agricultural College (now Michigan

State) in the late 19th century and wanted to figure out how she could use laboratory science techniques she learned there to help in the child-rearing process. Katharine had developed her own theory of personality type, labelling people as "meditative," "spontaneous," "executive," and "sociable." But, in 1932, she encountered Carl Jung's "Psychological Types," and used his ideas of "introversion versus extroversion" and "thinking versus feeling" as a new way to categorize people. Isabel, who had inherited her mother's interest in typological theory, then began designing the first prototype of the Myers-Briggs Indicator in the early 1940s.

In an interview, Merve was asked, "To what extent do businesses still use the Myers-Briggs system today?" Her answer is fascinating:

> It's really prolific. So, the most recent statistics indicate that 1 in every 5 Fortune 1,000 companies uses it in the hiring process. Eighty-nine of the Fortune 100 companies use it either in the hiring process, or in the workplace for team-building exercises, leadership coaching, executive talent management, things like that. The marketplace for workplace personality assessments is upwards of $2 billion. Many of the companies that publish and administer these indicators are private, so it's hard to know exactly what the market share of the Myers-Briggs Type Indicator is, but in the late '90s, it was estimated that their share would be about 25 to 30 percent of that market.[21]

Three of the top management consulting firms, McKinsey, Bain, and BCG, as well as two of the largest the world's consulting firms in the world (by number of employees) Deloitte and Accenture, use the Myers-Briggs test to help groups that are coming together to work on a project to better understand their team members. Projects tend to last a few months, and so teams are assembled to focus on a consulting client and the specific issue that the consultants are focused on based on their previous project experience, areas of expertise and also being available. Often, these teams are fairly unique, and the exact same team may never form again for another project, as people's availability may vary considerably over time. To help them come together as a team, one commonly used approach is to have people share their Myers-Briggs profiles so they can understand a bit about the person and have some insight into how they like to work. We have been told that the extrovert/introversion dimension is probably the one that is given the most attention. How do they work during the day, in teams, by themselves? In the evening, after a long, busy day, do they prefer as an introvert to go to their room and unwind with Netflix, or do they prefer as an extrovert to join in an optional team dinner?

Extroverts/Introverts, Medical Doctors, and Dentists

Karl has taught at McGill's medical school for a few years, he was appointed an associate professor there some years ago in appreciation of his work teaching leadership at the school for a range of physicians. Including residents (trainee doctors) as well as physicians with five to ten years' experience, and then senior physicians with over 25 years' experience. From many conversations on the topic, it appears that to a fair degree, doctors choose their speciality based on their personality. After their medical degree in Canada, and indeed much of the world, residents do rotations through a few different areas, areas that they get to choose.

In Canada and the US, medical residency after your medical degree typically lasts three to seven years, depending on your specialty. The shortest is family medicine, often three years or so. This is a generalist who is often the first line of defence of the medical system and sends patients on to specialists as it is appropriate. Which tends to call for more of an extroverted personality as you are seeing patients non-stop, often with family members with them. If you see a child as a patient, mom or/and dad is often there as well, understandably so. Meaning that there is often considerable social interaction as a family physician. On the other hand, the longest residencies are apt to be specialized surgical residencies, for example, neurosurgery and cardiac surgery, which top the list at six to eight years. Both of which are more apt to appeal to introverts because of the nature of your relationship with the patient. Of course, prestige, challenge and income are also other elements of deciding what speciality you choose.

The medical residents spend several months trying out in the area of medical practice, not just studying it as they do in medical school, but by being at the hospital or at a medical clinic working with long-term doctors to practice a speciality and get a sense of what they particularly prefer. After all, they are going to typically spend a lifetime practicing a speciality. It is in residency that doctors get to choose which speciality appeals to them. To some degree, personality matters in terms of a speciality. A number of new, medium, and long-term physicians have told Karl that they are family physicians because they are with people all day and this appeals to them as more extroverted people, on the other hand other hand there are a number of specialties like radiology, anesthesiologists, surgeons, non-clinical medical careers and perhaps most clearly, pathologists.[22] In these medical specialties, there is typically little interaction with patients. Unlike family physicians, radiologists and anesthesiologists typically deal with other physicians and little with patients. An anesthesiologist's main conversation with a patient is to ask them to start counting down from 100, and they sincerely hope the patient nods off around 95 or 94, and they will, if they have done their job well. For a pathologist, they often study samples from people and people who have died. Their important and critical job is to understand why, for a number of important reasons. These are vital medical roles that particularly appear to introverts.

Most dentists are family dentists and so have to act extroverted as they spend much of their day with a variety of people and have to explain what they are doing.[23] Specialists need to explain even more than a family dentist. Most patients would understand when a dentist fills a cavity, but what the specialist is doing is more unusual for the patients, and they spend considerable time explaining what they are doing and why.

Other factors enter in beyond personality, a sense of calling, helping people in great need and sometimes income matters too. Recently, someone told Karl that his wife (the other person) was partly a heart surgeon because it was better paid than a family physician. And there are other reasons as well.

Another healthcare expert suggested that the top five jobs for extroverts in healthcare were public health nurse, travel nurse, physical therapist, public relations and marketing personnel, and community health worker.[24] Joycelyn explains why she leads with a public health nurse,

> Public Health Nurses focus more on community health and wellness of the population than most nurses. Nurses often focus on one patient at a time, but public health nurses care and educate groups simultaneously. From testing to facilitating workshops on community health's importance to spreading health facts to school children, public health nurses are always moving and connecting.

Things that would often more typically appeal to extroverts.

Our Extrovert World and How It Came to Be

The extrovert's behaviour exhibits an outward-going nature, so their strengths are often easy to spot and therefore easily identifiable. Onlookers label extroverts as those who deliver inspiring speeches, schmooze within their social circles to achieve beneficial strategic objectives or determine and assert decisions as leaders during fast-paced crises.[25] Extroverts are confident in times of uncertainty—sometimes overly so. They can motivate their teams to rally around a common goal and can, in their better moments, captivate most of those with whom they come into contact. Thanks to their tendency to think aloud, they usually excel in on the fly, impromptu ventures and situations. These qualities allow executives to, in some sense, *perform* for their subordinates, board of directors, or clientele base. Extroverted charm also encourages meaningful connections and the establishment of strong networks.

Leadership in the past has often fallen to the loudest person in the room, or whoever is most adamant about their ability to guarantee success for the group. Extroverted executives are more apt to appear in control and competent at managing their role's challenges, particularly due to their external processing mechanisms that inform relevant parties of their concentration on potential issues. This method eases any stress or uncertainty experienced by stakeholders dependent on the organization's longevity, as they can palpably see and hear the company's leader taking action. Capable of assuming this position, extroverts are often found at the head of the conference table—according to Adam Grant, nearly all top-level leaders in 2010 (96%) were extroverted.[26]

Extroverts have often occupied positions in the White House, too—our jour-nalist friends confirmed this fact above. Additionally, in their study demonstrat-ing the link between dominance, perceived leadership, and competence, Young and French find that politically extroverted US presidents were more likely to earn public approval than those who were politically introverted.[27]

Why have we historically preferred extroverts to be our leaders? Susan Cain answers this question by pointing to the shift from the culture of character to the culture of personality that accompanied the rise of Industrial America. This era of urbanization and immigration transformed the average American's typical place to live and work from generational agricultural societies to cities. Sud-denly, neighbours were strangers instead of friends and family. It therefore became a necessity to build relationships with others despite a lack of civic or family ties, or of common heritage or upbringing. In this new setting of "increas-ingly anonymous business and social relationships . . . anything—including a first impression—had made [a] crucial difference." Faced with these pressures to build the same networks in new, more challenging circumstances, "Americans started to focus on how others perceived them."[28]

Initially promoted as strategies for businessmen to engage with strangers, the social qualities and "go-getter" attitude of naturally extroverted individuals became the solution to tackle this new predicament.[29] This eventually expanded beyond business and into the everyday engagements of all Americans; Cain points to these events as leading to the rise of the self-help and advertising indus-tries targeted at insecurities surrounding personality or physical appearance. It also promoted the rise of Hollywood movie stars who could seamlessly portray the ideal qualities of success in the culture of personality.

Given the preconceived notions of comfort that extroverts present, as well as their fit into our ideal personality mould and their ability to perform in social situations, it makes sense that we trust loud leaders and have built the foundation of our corporate structures in such a way that allows social butterflies to flourish.

Women and Extroversion

Since their gradual integration into the workforce around the mid-19th century, sparked by the industrial revolution, women have continually faced discrimina-tion and barriers in professional settings. This historical backdrop is essential for understanding the current landscape, especially regarding traits such as extro-version that are highly valued in the workplace. It is crucial to understand the relationship between gender and extroversion to understand how variations in extroversion (high or low) can influence the inequalities faced by women in the workplace and leadership roles.

Exploring gender differences in personality traits is key, though not without controversy. Much of the debate has revolved around the root cause of observed differences. The biological approach proposes that the differences in gender personality are rooted in our evolutionary past. According to this viewpoint, key factors that have influenced the development of personalities include issues related to reproduction (i.e., finding a mate) and the investments parents make in their offspring (such as the care, time, and resources devoted to ensuring their children's survival and success) that differ in men and women.[30] In contrast, sociocultural theories argue that gender norms, which dictate distinct societal roles for men and women, lead to divergent socialization processes.[31] It's plausible that both evolutionary and sociocultural dynamics contribute to gender differences.

In delving into the Big Five personality model, particularly the trait of extroversion, we encounter a nuanced conclusion. Despite the model's widespread recognition, it sometimes lacks depth in its analysis. By dissecting extroversion into two facets—enthusiasm and assertiveness—we can gain clearer insights into gender-related differences. Weisberg, DeYoung, and Hirsh (2011) notice a slight but significant gender difference in overall extroversion, with women scoring higher. When examining enthusiasm and assertiveness separately, however, a complex pattern emerges. Women tend to score higher in enthusiasm, reflecting greater sociability and positive emotions, whereas men typically excel in assertiveness, a trait associated with agency and leadership.[32]

This divergence becomes particularly relevant in male-dominated environments that value assertiveness and other similar leadership traits linked to extroversion. Although women may show higher overall levels of extraversion in enthusiasm, the professional emphasis on assertiveness and leadership traits tilts the scale in favour of men. This dynamic fosters stereotypes that fortify the challenges women face in professional and societal areas. Such stereotypes and biases necessitate a re-evaluation of the qualities valued in leadership and success, and call for a more inclusive understanding that appreciates the full spectrum of extroversion beyond traditionally masculine-coded traits.

The societal expectations of women have customarily valued traits associated with introversion, such as passivity, agreeableness, and a nurturing demeanour. These stereotypes have often confined women to roles that limit their visibility and influence in public and professional spheres. However, research shows that women who embody traits associated with extroverted leadership—like assertiveness and dominance—can transcend these norms, often at the risk of inciting backlash. Margaret Thatcher's rise to becoming the UK's first female Prime Minister exemplifies the power of assertiveness in overcoming sexism. Her extroverted and firm leadership style, which contrasted starkly with societal expectations, not only facilitated her political success but also challenged gendered stereotypes of leadership. Time Magazine encapsulates this sentiment by stating, "[Margaret] Thatcher's extroverted and firm personality helped her bull her way through British sexism to become the country's first female Prime Minister." Thatcher's tenure, marked by bold and assertive leadership, earning her the epithet of the "Iron Lady," illustrates the strategic use of extroversion by a woman to navigate a male-dominated political landscape.

Despite Thatcher's successes and her demonstration that assertive leadership can be independent of gender, women today still face challenges in portraying traditionally masculine leadership traits in the workplace. A systemic double standard and related vocabulary exist that reshape descriptions of the actions of female leaders if these actions are deemed to be *too* masculine. For instance, a woman who is assertive in her own opinions could be referred to as bossy and aggressive, while a man with the same belief about his own views goes unrecognized. Alternatively, women who do not challenge the socially acceptable mould of femininity might be called ladylike and vivacious. The dilemma women face in attempting to balance their feminine and masculine leadership traits in such a way that society might accept their efforts to become better leaders is convoluted and exhausting. For successfully combating this challenge on a daily basis in an attempt to dismantle this system, women in leadership roles are remarkably noteworthy.

Strength #1: Energy Effectors

If everyone gives a lot back, I can give even more—it's an exchange with the crowd.
Chahram Bolouri, Co-Founder of b.cycle
(Montréal Spin and Barre studio) and former
CEO Air Canada Technical Services

The extrovert exists in equilibrium with their external environment. They consistently interact with and react to social objects in their surroundings in exchanges that produce energy for them to undertake other tasks or responsibilities. Such interactions may involve sharing emotions, anecdotes, or humour, thereby allowing the extrovert to open up discussions with others and create a welcoming, positive social environment. As a fundamental tenet of extroversion, this strength is one that other extrovert strengths later build upon.

While studying social interactions between previously unacquainted undergraduate participants, SUNY's Eaton and UC Riverside's Funder determined positive affectivity to be correlated to extroversion; extroverts may use their affinity to engage with their environment to sponsor social communication and create a social press for positivity.[33] As they charge their own battery through social interaction, the extrovert uplifts others and creates an atmosphere that is warm and safe for all to participate in. Since this finding had materialized in a foreign setting with unknown individuals, it is likely to become further amplified as the extrovert fosters relationships with others in his or her environment. Moreover, others (even introverts) will become increasingly comfortable in the familiar, warm atmosphere, allowing for their more enthusiastic participation in interactions that, in turn, contribute further to energy production for the extrovert. This will create a feedback loop of positive energetic transmission, which enhances active engagement and increases the dynamic discussion of experiences and ideas, thus producing the potential for more refined, thorough results.

Paul Desmarais III, Chairman and CEO at Sagard Holdings, prefers to regenerate by engaging with a lively ambiance:

> What defines me as an extrovert is that I will spend three days with 300 people, wake up at 6 a.m. and go to bed at 2 a.m. at night all three of those days. I'll be energized for the next month as a result.

Desmarais represents this extrovert strength in action—a strong executive must set the tone of any room they enter, and this often requires a tireless ability to boost others around them with a few upbeat jokes or lighthearted stories before getting down to business. This act initiates the positive feedback loop of energy transfer. Extroverted figureheads can significantly improve the organization's social chemistry and bring extra energy to all levels within the group. The extrovert possesses the natural aura and emotional generosity to create an environment where everyone can feel comfortable and deepen their social ties. When they, themselves, are invigorated by this practice, executives can repeat this behaviour on a regular basis and consistently elevate their team environment for more inclusive discussion.

Everyone loves a personality hire. Known as such because their strongest skills are associated with their charismatic and friendly personality, this group of individuals are useful hires to recruiters in that they can improve morale in the workplace and assist in building relationships with clients. They make the office a great place to be every day. Extroverts, obviously, are perfect for this role. It is another way their energy effector strength manifests to benefit those around them. Through the creation of positive energy around them, in their better moments, extroverts lighten the mood, better the work culture, and help everyone enjoy themselves more at the office.

This strength is somewhat unique to extroverts, as introverts are known to expend energy rather than create it when engaging with their external environment. As a result, they are less adept at the dynamics of this practice.

There are two important caveats to extroverts' positive feedback loop of energy: first, for the greatest benefit, it is necessary for others in the environment to respond and react appropriately to the extrovert's energy release; second, the extrovert must remain sensitive to those around them during this process. It is not all good; extroverts must be aware of the potential downsides and learn to mitigate them.

The extrovert's ideal surroundings are ones which strongly reinforce the energy he or she releases via appropriate responses. If others engage with and react to them, the extrovert will become capable of ensuring a positive atmosphere. Although the extrovert will usually sustain some level of this strength regardless of a supporting presence, its benefits are maximized in a setting which engages, values and rewards their efforts.

Just as others should remain aware of the needs of the extrovert, the extrovert must read those around them and become attuned to the energy levels of others. This is necessary for the extrovert to appropriately gauge how to best uplift their audience. Often, this task presents a significant challenge to the extrovert; it is associated with an inherent weakness of the communication style, something that will be discussed later in this chapter.

Strength #2: Masters of the Social Network

I like the conversation and I like to participate in it. I'm not shy to say this, it's a two-way street: I like people, but I also want them to like me.

Mitch Garber (Canadian Lawyer, Investor, and CEO; Chairman of Cirque du Soleil, Co-owner of the Seattle Kraken NHL team)

Networking is very, very important in today's world. Gino, Kouchaki, and Casciaro (2016) argue that professional networks lead to greater opportunities, deeper knowledge, greater innovation, faster advancement, and higher status and authority levels.[34] Their study, focused on 165 lawyers in a North American-based firm, confirms that success (defined in this case by bringing clients to the firm and earning assignments to premium client accounts) depends on the lawyer's ability to network effectively both outside and within the firm.

In its better moments, extroverted charm sponsors the formation of meaningful connections. Authentic engagement with others in the extrovert's external environment creates bonds and the foundations for beneficial relationships. In this context, the result of an effective use of Strength #1 allows the extrovert's social network to develop and flourish.

Duke University's Duffy and Chartrand assert that extroverts build rapport better than introverts, a skill vital to the establishment of a strong network.[35] What behaviours do extroverts undertake to connect with others more effectively? Besides the more explicit active engagement (via energy transfers) with those around them, Duffy and Chartrand claim that if the extrovert is motivated to affiliate with certain individuals, they will increase mimicry of these individuals as a means to build rapport. One may view this behaviour as a strategy to appear more familiar, welcoming, and less threatening to the new individual in the hopes of forming a bond (like the outcome of Strength #1).

We should also mention an additional, and rather interesting, result of Duffy and Chartrand's study: extroverts' social skills are utilized only in the event of a reward, such as potential affiliation with a certain individual. Instead of enjoying the social mechanism itself, extroverts are usually more receptive to rewards and use social mechanisms as a vehicle to achieve such awards. In other words, the extrovert enjoys the result of a formed bond more than the process of forming bonds—a peculiar finding which allows us greater insight into the extroverted mind. The extrovert loves their network and its benefits, although building it is a slightly less thrilling ordeal.

Heather Chalmers, President and CEO of General Electric Canada, is one to appreciate the value of her relationships beyond the benefits cited by Duffy and Chartrand: "Networking takes on a different meaning where I am now. It is a gift to constantly hear what others think, gaining a little bit of insight in these disparate conversations."

Chalmers's network is a reservoir of creative and diverse individuals by whom she can run her ideas. Through listening to, learning, and discussing these ideas, Chalmers will have an epiphany, "that one moment, where you will say, oh my! There is the missing piece of the puzzle that I needed to move that strategy forward!"

This connects with Henry Mintzberg's idea of emergent strategy, which stands in contrast to Michael Porter's more deliberate or top-down strategy. From many, many CEO conversations, the reality is that both approaches are used to some degree in most organizations. But in today's more turbulent world, the idea is that strategy comes to a considerable degree from front-line troops who are fully immersed in the real world of customers, suppliers, and competitors. Senior management still decides the strategy, but increasingly with input from much more junior people. As a result, strategy makers must be better at listening than in the past. Networking and talking with employees are more and more vital, yet learning to listen may be a challenge for some extroverts and come naturally to introverts. More on this later in Chapter 5.

Networks offer significant advantages. Since extroverts excel at building their web of connections, they are more likely than introverts to reap these great benefits in future endeavours. Point for the extrovert!

Strength #3: Confidence During Crisis

> If you are leading something, you're trying to manage the crisis. You, the extrovert feature, are often called forth.
>
> Dick Pound (Former International Olympic Committee Member, two time Olympic champion and often the public face of the Olympics worldwide)

Extroverts exude confidence and tend to stand out in a crowd. In times of uncertainty, a confident and assuring leader is exactly what a group needs to direct strategy and inspire the troops. Bolton of Imperial College, Princeton's Brunnermeier, and Columbia's Veldkamp find that more "resolute, steadfast CEOs who stick to their guns" tend to be better leaders.[36] These results are also consistent with Gervais, Heaton, and Odean, who examined the conditions under which overconfident CEOs perform better.[37] Our world has been constructed for extrovert leadership precisely because they seem competent and reliable at handling crises—they are loud, they are confident, and they let everyone know they have a plan to fix the issue. Stakeholders trust them to lead.

Paul Sislian, Executive VP of Operations and Operational Excellence at Bombardier Aviation believes the decisive nature associated with extroverted confidence is a strong asset: "I'm an extrovert. Analysis paralysis really exists, because there are some people who will overanalyze, and as they're overanalyzing, life is moving by. My life is moving!"

Paralysis by analysis, as Paul calls it, is often experienced in businesses that are not moving in times when they should move.

Why do extroverts seem more decisive? It is not because they make decisions faster—in fact, research suggests that the brain of the introvert processes thoughts faster than that of the extrovert; since introverts think in a more internalized fashion, their brains are well-practiced and efficient at processing and concluding on ideas.[38] The extrovert tends to think all over the place. They immediately articulate partially processed results as opinions or streams of consciousness, which they then gather and organize aloud, from a disparate series of thoughts into one finalized conclusion.[39] Observing this process may give a viewer the impression of decisiveness on behalf of the extrovert—watching the extrovert talk themselves through a problem and witnessing their reasoning at each step provides a greater understanding of how point B was deduced from point A. For introverts, this process occurs internally, with only the decision being presented, thus leaving room for others to question the logic of the introvert's deductions, since they are implied rather than explicitly stated. The introvert may be ambiguous, while the extrovert is definitive and clear. Combined with their characteristic certainty, the extrovert's decisiveness is evident.

The extrovert executive appears capable of managing the challenges of their organization as a direct result of their decisiveness. As we suggested previously, extroverts talk to think through their decisions. Conversational deliberation of ideas allows thorough processing to occur out loud and with subordinates or team members; because there is greater involvement of other skilled minds, live discussion and assessment of ideas is sometimes more fruitful than what would occur if each participant finalized decisions on their own before bringing them to the team for presentation (as would likely be the case with a group of introverts). Each participant exhibits a varied perception and a unique view on the factors involved in the issue at hand. Consistent discussion and debate through the thought process ensures greater accuracy at each stage.

Although Biers and Hackman produced no significant differences in performance across single and group conditions, their study determined that group conditions are more efficient for extracting high-value information.[40] We believe this deduction is powerful. It should be mentioned that Biers and Hackman centred their study around six structured tasks. The ability of a team to derive and infer valuable conclusions by working aloud with one another is an asset far more beneficial in a setting that lacks structure and is fraught with uncertainty—such as a crisis, for instance. Talking through a problem, as extroverts prefer to do, might illuminate previously under-considered details in such a way that would not occur without group deliberation. In times of crisis, these tidbits could mean the difference between success and failure for the team. Talking through it involves a number of people and often gives a greater sense of confidence in the group about the final decision on how to move forward.

Another positive outcome of this mechanism is a greater capacity for the extrovert to improvise or to think on their feet. Whereas introverts typically need to internally produce an idea before presenting it, extroverts make decisions fast and aloud. They can simultaneously present their ideas with certainty and confidence while forming them, a key component of skilled improvisation. When their idea is sound (which, hopefully, it always is), this strength is often a highly efficient asset for their company.

Strength #4: Natural Motivational Speakers

> Energy! We get conversations going. If you're doing it right, you are trying to pull in the introverts as well.
>
> Heather Chalmers (President and CEO, General Electric Canada)

Extroverts are masters of social energy. Since they are always undertaking energy interactions with their surroundings, they have become adept at feeling energy dynamics and raising energy levels. They use communication to drive this energy upwards, oftentimes by taking charge of the group and delivering a joke or anecdote to reel in the crowd. As discussed under Strength #1, extroverts know how to set the tone of a meeting, a dinner, or a conversation. They usually know exactly what to say to accomplish their goal. The extrovert who is highly skilled at this strength will be capable of working a room, using its dynamics to their advantage; the extrovert ensures the inclusion of all involved, including the introverts, as they elevate the atmosphere.

In another context, extroverts may turn their energy virtuosity into eloquent and uplifting speeches. There is nothing quite like the feeling that comes from listening to an inspiring delivery. We have all been there—in the midst of a grand feat, on the verge of admitting failure and searching for a reason to keep going. At this moment, we require advice and support from a mentor figure to motivate us. They remind us to persist until our goal is reached or the issue is tackled. In times like these, the extrovert is often well-equipped to act as the fountain of inspiration we need. JP Gagne, CEO of AI giant ElementAI, agrees: "It is all about being clear, crisp, and connected at the moment."

According to Pendleton and Furnham, inspirers must feel comfortable with people and be keen to communicate.[41] The extrovert excels at giving motivational speeches—their well-seasoned abilities to connect with others, engage with their social surroundings, go off script and think on the fly if necessary or appropriate and be comfortable with public speaking are all qualities that help them articulate a meaningful, authentic, and awe-inspiring delivery. The extrovert may use this skill in a wide range of circumstances as a corporate executive, including at board meetings to drive a strategy forward, in front of crowds to promote a company image, pitching a group of Wall Street analysts, an annual meeting, or in a room of employees as the company faces a particularly challenging or stressful situation.

In one of our more recent interviews, we encountered an executive who disagreed with our assessment of the importance of the inspiring speech. We found this divergence to be rather interesting, given the executive ran a world-class sports team—an organization where, generally, we perceived the inspiring speech as a quintessential component of a coach's toolkit.

According to Mark Shapiro, CEO of the Toronto Blue Jays,

Inspiring speeches are a little bit of a fallacy . . . being inspiring is short-lived. If I am setting the tone for the values of the organization, then I am doing a better job than I am giving a rah-rah speech.

Without values, an executive holds no authenticity—a vital component of effective leadership in today's world, more than ever. This is a theme that Karl has heard again and again in his weekly CEO interviews, particularly since the pandemic. As CEO of the Toronto Blue Jays baseball team, Shapiro's role is to establish the values of the organization. Once cemented, these tenets should be integrated into the daily operations of the company, and thus, there is often no need for a "rah-rah speech" to get everyone going. If a CEO does their job correctly, the "rah-rah speech," although always well received, should become an uncommon occurrence. An interesting take that resonates with us.

The Hill Times, a Canadian newspaper which covers the Parliament of Canada and the Canadian federal government, recently had an article entitled, "The authenticity game." It argued that "It's hard to avoid the conclusion that talking a good populist game is more politically advantageous than any agenda devoted to actually improving peoples' lives." "Politicians like Conservative Leader Pierre Poilievre, and Ontario Premier Doug Ford have an advantage when voters care more about the perception of an official as honest rather than likable".[42] These are Canadian examples; American politics clearly also supports this finding. Kamala Harris was seen as trying to be authentic to voters. She did have some success, as many observers commented on her ability to connect on a personal level with people she meets. *The Observer* newspaper in the UK was just one of many which commented, "she radiates joy, humour and humility."[43] With consideration of the election's outcome and a popular victory to Donald Trump, however, perhaps perceived honesty of populism won out this time. In *Policy*

Options, political professor Lori Turnbull wrote, in February 2023, "The concept of authenticity can be unpacked in different ways depending on the circumstances but, in politics, to be authentic is to say what you mean and to live the true version of yourself regardless of who is watching."[44]

We prefer to view the "rah-rah speech" as a way to remind team members of company values in those (hopefully rare) tumultuous and difficulty-laden circumstances. We believe that key players benefit from the reinforcement of company ideals related to purpose, priorities, and what is important. These team members also gain from any elevated energy the extroverted leader may provide by boosting the atmosphere during their address. Therefore, although it is not needed as in the past, if the executive has built a proper foundation for the organization, we recommend keeping this strength in the tool chest for extraordinary times. The extrovert will know what to do with it.

Strength #5: Transformational Leaders

In many respects, the best time to affect transformational change is when our back is against the wall. That's the time that we see the greatest creativity, the greatest strengths, and the greatest commitment from the people that needed to participate in this transformation.

Calin Rovinescu (CEO of Air Canada, 2009–2021,
who led very considerable change at Air Canada)

Transformational leadership aims to cause a change in social systems and people. Initially introduced by James MacGregor Burns in 1978 to describe political leaders, the business world has since adopted this term to better understand optimal corporate leadership.[45] Transformational leaders must align their teams, motivate and inspire, and establish direction.[46] The resulting change is often dramatic.

Psychologists Bono and Judge assessed personality traits related to three dimensions of transformational leadership (charisma, intellectual stimulation, and individualized consideration) and three dimensions of transactional leadership (contingent reward, active management by exception, and passive leadership).[47] They found stable extroversion to be the most consistent correlate of transformational leadership. Zopiatis and Constantini (2018) produced a similar result in their research: their results showed that transformational leadership is positively associated with extraversion.[48]

Leaders at the forefront of a transformation must utilize all the aforementioned strengths of extroverts to enact systemic or social change. As Rovinescu described, the need for transformational leadership often arises during situations where everything seems to be going wrong. Faults with the current system are causing failure—the need for change is dire and increasing, but such change must be launched and managed effectively. The extrovert is prepared to handle such stress—they are confident, calm, and collected; they work aloud and show others that the problem is being addressed (Strength #3); they empower others with words and elevates the team's energy if necessary (Strength #1, 4); and they will likely maintain a strong network of individuals that support them and may assist the team if in dire need (Strength #2).

Air Canada is a story of transformation that Karl watched closely. In 2010 through 2012, Karl gave a two-day course at Air Canada on being a change leader for 20 senior managers at a time. He recited this lecture 12 times across Canada, presenting to a total of 240 senior managers at Air Canada, many now running the company. He also ran an advanced leadership programme with his colleague Henry Mintzberg, including round tables of six executives from Air Canada. A central part of the three-module programme was working on a group change project. In early 2009, Calin Rovinescu, who, after four years as a senior executive at Air Canada, was working as an Investment Banker at Genuity Capital. Calin and Karl had agreed to teach a course on leading change for the McGill MBA. Rather than teach the theory, Calin ended up rejoining Air Canada as CEO in 2009 to take it through great industry-leading change.

Since that time, Karl has commented very frequently on Air Canada and other airlines like WestJet, Porter Airlines, Transat, etc. and how they have fared. High fuel prices, increased competition, low-cost carriers, and the growing importance of global alliances all caused great stress for the airline industry, of course, including Air Canada.

Probably the time of greatest crisis for airlines was the COVID years, when over 90% of business disappeared and many airlines faced extinction. On his hour-long radio show, Karl has interviewed the last four CEOs of Air Canada, the last and current CEOs of WestJet, the current and first CEO of Porter Airlines, all in Canada and the CEO of Air France, Air Baltic, one of the Lufthansa airlines, etc. Karl has made a point to ask about this uncertain period.

In the airline industry, Air Canada and several other major airlines have undergone significant transformation, with many experiencing bankruptcies. Calin and other airline leaders demonstrated strong leadership to transform their airlines, and collectively through the Star Alliance, One World, and Sky Team, the industry.

This undertaking called for strong transformational leadership.

Shortcomings of the Extrovert

Although they possess many attractive qualities for success in today's organizational structures, extroverts are, of course, imperfect. The same qualities which allow extroverts to thrive on some occasions can also create a negative in other circumstances. For instance, although extroverted confidence and assertiveness help to promote one's opinions among other employees and increase chances of success in the boardroom, they might also coincide with reduced listening, reduced open-mindedness, and being less collaborative. To balance the books a bit, what follows is a description of the extrovert's key shortcomings and the potential negative effects these weaknesses may have in the workplace.

Weakness #1: Lower Self-Reflection and Self-Awareness Skills

> I would say for the most part, I feel extroverted, but it really depends on the situation. I actually started to feel, as I got older, a little more introverted. But I think it also might just be because I realize I don't know everything.
>
> Erin Little (Co-founder at startup Landish Foods)

There comes a price to pay for the extrovert's way of engaging with their environment rather than with themselves. Because the extrovert processes thoughts externally or *speaks to think*, they will express a variety of opinions before circling back to a finalized conclusion on the relevant issue. We have already established that this can be a strength in this external deliberation process; however, there are some key weaknesses we must mention as well.

Firstly, this process is vulnerable to its environment. Introverted reflection always occurs under the same internal conditions, so the process is consistent and produces relatively dependable results. The extrovert process, on the other hand, takes place in diverse environments with different people and audiences each time, which may lead to more variable results. It can depend too much on whom you run into as opposed to the deliberate internal thought processes of introverts, which typically work more consistently. Sometimes a strategy is best put together with considerable conscious thought about who are the right people to get input from. People who are quite knowledgeable of the customer, the supplier, and the competitors understand where the world is going, so we adjust our strategy to today's world, rather than keep ploughing ahead with a strategy better suited to yesterday's world.

A 2024 article by McKinsey asked the question, "Is the World Facing a State of Permacrisis?" of two leading economists, Michael Spence of Stanford, Mohamed El-Erian, president of Queens' College Cambridge, who with former UK Chancellor of the Exchequer and Prime Minister Gordon Brown, wrote a book, *Permacrisis*. The title may be a bit over the top, nevertheless the idea that we live in more turbulent times is one that seems to be widely held. We agree with Michael's final point in the piece, "You have to engage with this stuff." Engaging for the extrovert may well mean getting to a wider their normal audience and really, truly listening, in order to put together today's way forward.

Secondly, the extrovert is significantly less introspective than their introverted counterpart. The extrovert becomes less seasoned in the practice of looking inwards to reflect, and less practiced self-reflection has its consequences: failing to think sufficiently before speaking, a greater focus on the self as opposed to others, less humility, and a generally weaker self-awareness.

Self-awareness is a prerequisite for improvement, or knowing when one should change. Therefore, its absence could pose potential concerns of catastrophic magnitude—ones which might frustrate team members and deter them from collaborative work at the organization. The effects of potentially weaker self-awareness will become evident in the discussion of the next two weaknesses. For many, self-awareness is a prerequisite for senior leaders in today's world.

According to Brandi Halls, Director of Brand Communications at Lush Cosmetics, this realization might also have to occur in the transition from employee to executive, when the primary focus shifts from personal success to the joint success of a team:

> You know, you spend most of your career really trying to sort of get noticed and progress your career through that. One of my biggest leadership learnings, that I had to learn the hard way, was that it's not about me anymore. It's about my team. It's about me being set up to lead a team. But it's not necessarily about my work or my output anymore.

Weakness #2: Dominating Instead of Listening

> I think any extrovert, if they're going to be good in leadership, working with teams, you have to be prepared to listen as well.
> Willie Walsh (Director of IATA, ex-CEO of British Airways)

We have established that the extrovert knows how to work the room. But are they actively engaged with those around them? Zlatev, Flynn, and Collins' research suggests that people often perceive extroverts as inauthentic, adopting personas to suit their situation, and less interested in the thoughts and feelings of others.[49] People feel this way about the extrovert because sometimes it seems like they are not listening. Across six studies and 2500 participants, the team discovered that the interaction partners of extroverts consistently judge extroverts to be worse listeners who assume inauthentic personas to fit the circumstance.[50]

Extroverts have earned the reputation of being poor listeners. Strength #2 mentions Duffy and Chartrand's study, which found that extroverts enjoyed the perks of a bond itself rather than the process of forming said bond.[51] Perhaps this means that the extrovert, distracted by the objective to expand their network and form a meaningful connection, may not be fully engaged with the social interaction itself. As a result, it is possible that they are not listening as attentively to others speaking as they are to themselves; the average extrovert could probably stand to listen a little bit better to their peers.

"The Dalai Lama said when you speak, you are going to learn nothing. But when you listen, there's a chance you might learn something." Daniel Borsuk, Plastic Surgeon in Montréal, after quoting this statement, explained, "I'm more of an extrovert, but wish sometimes that I was more of an introvert."

In all the interactions the extrovert initiates with their surroundings, they are inevitably on the sending or receiving end of the transaction. Therefore, they participate at least half of the time, usually with their own views or experiences. As the extrovert grows accustomed to this role, it becomes an increasingly difficult one to share. If not careful, the extrovert will find themselves always needing to speak (mostly about themselves) and constantly seeking attention or a response from others. If another individual ever tries to share this spotlight, this extrovert and their now vulnerable ego are at risk of defending their territory in a distasteful manner.

Therefore, it is crucial to keep in mind that extrovert commanders need to make space and energy for the other people, especially introverts, to express themselves and to create a safe space where everyone, regardless of personality type, will feel fully comfortable sharing their own thoughts. As extroverts, they are in the best position to accomplish this objective.

Weakness #3: Lacking Situational Awareness

> You know, I think [introverts] listen. I think they observe better. When they speak, they tend to be a little bit more measured.
>
> Paul Desmarais III, CEO (Sagard Holdings)

Self-awareness and awareness of one's surroundings are highly complementary skills. Therefore, an extrovert lacking self-awareness might also lack external awareness as well—and this flaw can be an important one. The extrovert who lacks awareness will not seriously consider the opinions, sentiments, or needs of others. These qualities may harm the group chemistry and energy dynamics that this extrovert worked so hard to establish. Lacking awareness can be a detriment to the extrovert in several contexts.

Although the extrovert is actively engaged in their external environment, if their awareness skills are poor, they may not correctly perceive a given situation. Awareness composes the core of basic social skills—it is vital to understand the cues of others.

When surrounded by others, we are given the opportunity to build relationships by listening to them and earning their approval. Tim Murdoch, Head Coach of McGill Men's Lacrosse, believes that "[one] needs to learn and listen better, to look for signals indicating what is going on around. People stop listening at some point if they feel unheard."

We will also benefit from what we hear others say and what we think of these contributions. David Segal, co-founder of David's Tea, sometimes finds it challenging to observe others:

> Drive yourself crazy and let your thoughts get the better of you and just be able to and to sit with yourself and be with yourself and learn to have that awareness of your thoughts and develop that patience to not always react.

The absence of awareness brings hesitancy in self-development. Changing oneself requires internal reflection and the realization that areas for internal improvement exist. The extrovert's confidence and certainty in themselves and their ideas make it increasingly difficult to adjust behaviours. This persona may make it more challenging for them to look at things outside of their own normal scope and social processes, potentially preventing essential changes from occurring.

Our Key Takeaways

#1 Extroverts require less effort to fit into C-suite level jobs because at the surface, the skill requirements for executives often align seamlessly with their natural tendencies and strengths.

We have established that our corporate world is one that has traditionally been built for more noisy leaders. As motivational speakers, social butterflies, and energy elevators, extroverts can earn public approval more easily. Extrovert executives process situations externally in such a manner that eases many relevant stakeholders' uncertainties. The assured confidence and authority that naturally exudes from the extrovert serve them well in this environment. In a culture of personality, extroverts are well-equipped performers capable of wooing their audience of subordinates, board directors, or clients. Basic corporate job requirements, such as leading a team, public speaking, and maintaining the company image, are well-aligned with the aforementioned extroverted qualities. With the corporate structure having been essentially built for them, extroverts adjust into the role of executive seamlessly and with great ease. But they need to be more aware, hence our second and third points.

#2 Extrovert energy is a double-edged sword: when positively reinforced, they provide considerably more than they receive; however, they require considerable positive feedback in order to sustain their energy necessary to operate in this manner.

The extrovert possesses the natural aura and emotional generosity to create an environment of strong social chemistry. To get the optimal benefit of this practice, it is very helpful for others in the environment to respond and react appropriately to the extrovert's energy release. Others should engage with the energy released by the extrovert so that he or she will become capable of ensuring a positive atmosphere. On the positive side, an extrovert's network can provide extroverts with a heightened external self-awareness that will allow them to become more self-reflective and learn to leverage this strength to their advantage. An important topic is how to manage upward, we will talk about this more later. If you work for an extrovert, you can be of considerable help to them by learning to help them maintain their energy levels.

#3 The ability of an extrovert to lead successfully is dependent on their self/external awareness and capability to gauge potential negative impacts associated with their leadership personality.

An extrovert lacking self-awareness or external awareness will not succeed. The extrovert who lacks such awareness will not think to hear the opinions of others. They are also unable to read social cues vital to making others in the group feel heard. These outcomes may harm the group chemistry and energy dynamics, deterring relationship building or work productivity. The extrovert must strive to remain aware of themselves and their surroundings. They must be mindful of their potential or actual impact on others, especially in a group with meeker or introverted personalities. Just as others should remain aware of the needs of the extrovert, the extrovert must read those around them and become attuned to the energy levels of others. This is a necessary skill to allow the extrovert to appropriately gauge how to best uplift their audience, or whether they should back off and leave a situation alone. The extrovert poses a risk of overpowering the group and antagonizing their peers if they are not careful with their influence.

Notes

1 Rampton, John. "10 U.S. Presidents Who Were Introverts." *Inc.*, August 21, 2015.
2 Hudson, Swinton W., and Ferguson, Jr., Geremy C. "Leadership Personalities: Extrovert, Introvert or Ambivert?" *The International Journal of Management* 2, no. 9 (2016): 999–1002.
3 Moore, Karl. "Two Days with Warren Buffett: Three Lessons from An Introverted Leader in Action." *Forbes.com*, May 5, 2017.
4 Stephens-Craig, D., Kuofie, M., and Dool, R. "Perception of Introverted Leaders by Mid to High-Level Leaders." *Journal of Marketing and Management* 6, no. 1 (2015): 62–75. Investigates the interplay of introversion and extroversion in leadership. Through investigation of mid to high-level leaders' perception of introversion, the study aims to connect positive traits of introverts to desirable leadership roles. The research emphasizes the need to recognize and value the contributions of introverted leaders, challenging traditional biases in favour of extroverted leadership traits in the workplace.

5 Stephens-Craig, D., Kuofie, M., and Dool, R. (2015). Carl Jung (1923, cf. infra.) emphasized the necessity of mutual psychological understanding when these two types interact, whether in personal relationships or professional settings. Translating this to the modern context, the paper argues that society has predominantly tailored itself to extroverted norms, often compelling introverts to adapt to an extroverted worldview. This forced adaptation can lead to internal conflict and may hinder introverts from realizing their full potential. Instead of pressuring introverted leaders to conform to extroverted stereotypes, the paper advocates for recognizing and nurturing the unique strengths and potential of introverts in the workplace. In their report on the assessment of introverted leaders by other leaders, Stephens-Craig, Kuofie, and Dool argue that modern corporate structures and norms favour the extroverted personality, circumstances that might "cause conflict and perhaps cripple [introverts'] ability to live up to their full potential (2015: 63)." In a later chapter, we will explore the effects of systemic disadvantages that introverts experience in the workplace and their unique strengths. From here, the importance of flexibility and balance in communication will become evident. Firstly, however, we must begin our analysis with an appreciation of our current system and its primary beneficiaries, extroverts, though *The Times They Are A-Changin'* (to quote a Bob Dylan song).
6 Stephens-Craig, D., Kuofie, M., and Dool, R. (2015).
7 Jung, Carl Gustav. *Collected Works of C.G. Jung, Volume 6: Psychological Types*, edited by Gerhard Adler and R.F.C. Hull, 563. Reprint, Princeton: Princeton University Press, 1923 [2014].
8 Jung, Carl Gustav. (1923).
9 Jung, Carl Gustav. (1923).
10 Jung, Carl Gustav. (1923): 564.
11 Jung, Carl Gustav. (1923).
12 Laney, Marti Olsen. *The Introvert Advantage: How Quiet People Can Thrive in an Extrovert World.* New York: Workman Publishing Company, 2002. Dr. Marti Olsen Laney explores the strengths and challenges of introverts, debunking common misconceptions. The book provides insights and strategies for introverts to navigate an extroverted world, emphasizing the value of their unique abilities in various life aspects.
13 Laney, Marti Olsen. (2002).
14 Laney, Marti Olsen. (2002).
15 Laney, Marti Olsen. (2002).
16 Hill, S. Y. and Yuan, H. "Familial Density of Alcoholism and Onset of Adolescent Drinking." *Journal of Studies on Alcohol* 60, no. 1 (1999): 7–17. https://doi.org/10.15288/jsa.1999.60.7; Cook, M., Young, A., Taylor, D., and Bedford, A. P. "Personality Correlates of Alcohol Consumption." *Personality and Individual Differences* 24, no. 5 (1998): 641–647. https://doi.org/10.1016/S0191–8869(97)00214–6.
17 Laney, Marti Olsen. (2002). Primary blood pathway in the brain requires dopamine for regulation. Dr. Laney posits that extroverts are less sensitive to dopamine, categorizing them as high-novelty seekers. Citing a study by Hamer of the National Cancer Institute, she explains that these individuals need thrilling experiences and constant change to maintain adequate dopamine levels. They tend to avoid routine tasks and are more inclined to seek dopamine-inducing experiences in their external environment, contrasting with introverts, who might feel overwhelmed by such interactions.
18 Brown, Sarah and Taylor, Karl. "Household Finances and the Big Five Personality Traits." *Journal of Economic Psychology* 45 (2014): 197–212. Personality traits are classified according to the "Big Five" taxonomy: openness to experience, conscientiousness, extraversion, agreeableness and neuroticism. We explore personality traits

at the individual level and also within couples, specifically the personality traits of the head of household and personality traits averaged across the couple. We find that certain personality traits, such as extraversion, are generally significantly associated with household finances in terms of the levels of debt and assets held, and the correlation is often relatively large. The results also suggest that the magnitude and statistical significance of the association between personality traits and household finances differ across the various types of debt and assets held in the household portfolio.

19   Stephens-Davidowitz, Seth and Greenberg, Lyle. "Personality Tests Aren't All the Same. Some Work Better Than Others." *Scientific American*, February 28, 2024.

20   Merve, Emre. *The Personality Brokers: The Strange History of Myers-Briggs and the Birth of Personality Testing.* New York: Houghton Mifflin Harcourt, 2018.

21   Nguyen, Janet. "How Companies Use the Myers-Briggs System to Evaluate Employees." *Marketplace*, October 30, 2018.

22   Jubball, Kevin. "Top Five Doctor Specialties for Introverts." *Med School Insider*, October 22, 2022.

23   Rodriguez, Kristan D., Bartoloni, Joseph A., and Hendricson, William D. "Is Dental Students' Clinical Productivity Associated with Their Personality Profile?" *Journal of Dental Education* 81, no. 12 (December 2017): 1436–1443.

     A bit older study is: Fenlon, Michael R., et al. "Personality of Dental Students in Two Dental Schools in the United Kingdom and in Ireland." *European Journal of Dental Education*, July 2008.

     Interestingly, a study of Chinese dentists found the majority to be introverts. Wu, Shengjun, et al. "Personality Types of Chinese Dental School Applicants." *Journal of Dental Education*, December 2007.

24   Ghansah, Joycelyn. "The 5 Best Healthcare Jobs for Extroverts." *Medjobs.co*, August 20, 2020.

25   Stephens-Craig, D., Kuofie, M., and Dool, R. "Perception of Introverted Leaders by Mid to High-Level Leaders." *Journal of Marketing and Management* 6, no. 1 (2015): 62–75.

26   Grant, Adam, Gino, Francesca, and Hofmann, David A. "Reversing the Extraverted Leadership Advantage: The Role of Employee Proactivity." *Academy of Management Journal* 54 (2011): 528–550. Extraversion is linked to leadership emergence and effectiveness. However, this paper argues that the impact of extraverted leadership on group performance varies based on employee behaviour. Dominance complementarity theory suggests that while extroverted leaders boost performance in passive employee groups, they may hinder proactive groups due to their reduced receptiveness to proactive behaviours. This was observed in two studies: one in pizza stores, where profits varied based on leader extraversion and employee proactivity, and another in a lab setting, confirming these findings. The research underscores the importance of matching leadership style with employee behaviour for optimal performance.

27   Young, T. J. and French, L. A. "Judged Political Extroversion-Introversion and Perceived Competence of US Presidents." *Perceptual and Motor Skills* 83, no. 2 (1996): 578–578. Politically extroverted US presidents (n = 20) were more likely to be ranked as "above average" in the Murray-Blessing poll than those judged as politically introverted (n = 15), and this is consistent with previous research on dominance and perceived leadership.

28   Cain, Susan. *Quiet: The Power of Introverts in a World That Can't Stop Talking*, 74. New York: Crown Publishing Group, 2012. The book delves into the historical shift in Western culture from valuing character to prioritizing personality, with a prevailing "extrovert ideal." Using scientific perspectives, the book highlights the misconceptions surrounding introversion, emphasizing its normalcy and prevalence.

It showcases that many influential figures in history were introverts. Cain advocates for societal changes to accommodate both temperaments and provides guidance for introverts navigating an extrovert-centric world, as well as advice for effective communication between different temperaments.

29 Cain, Susan. (2012).
30 Trivers, Robert L. "Parental Investment and Sexual Selection." In *Sexual Selection and the Descent of Man*, edited by Bernard Campbell, 136–179. Chicago: Aldine, 1972.
31 Wood, Wendy and Eagly, Alice H. "A Cross-Cultural Analysis of the Behavior of Women and Men: Implications for the Origins of Sex Differences." *Psychological Bulletin* 128, no. 5 (2002): 699–727.
32 Weisberg, Yanna J., DeYoung, Colin G., and Hirsh, Jacob B. "Gender Differences in Personality across the Ten Aspects of the Big Five." *Frontiers in Psychology* 2 (2011).
33 Eaton, Leslie G. and Funder, David C. "The Creation and Consequences of the Social World: An Interactional Analysis of Extraversion." *European Journal of Personality* 17, no. 5 (2003): 375–395.
34 Gino, Francesca, Kouchaki, Maryam, and Casciaro, Tiziana. "Learn to Love Networking." *Harvard Business Review*, May 2016.
35 Duffy, Kathleen A. and Chartrand, Tanya L. "The Extravert Advantage: How and When Extraverts Build Rapport with Other People." *Psychological Science* 26, no. 11 (2015): 1795–1802. Argues that extroverts build better rapport than introverts through mimicking behaviours. This skillfulness was assessed through two studies. In the first study, extraversion predicted increased mimicry only when an affiliation goal was present, not when it was absent. In study 2, mimicry seemed to mediate the relationship between extraversion and rapport, but only when an affiliation goal was present. The study argues that this skillfulness of extraverts emerges only when they are motivated to affiliate, providing evidence in favour of the reward-sensitivity-as-core model of extraversion over the sociability-as-core model of extraversion.
36 Bolton, Patrick, Brunnermeier, Markus Konrad, and Veldkamp, Laura. "Leadership, Coordination, and Mission-Driven Management." *AFA 2009 San Francisco Meetings Paper,* 2008.
37 Gervais, Simon, Heaton, J. B., and Odean, Terrance. "Overconfidence, Compensation Contracts, and Capital Budgeting." *The Journal of Finance* 66 (2011): 1735–1777.
38 Cooper, Belle Beth. "Are You an Introvert or an Extrovert? What It Means for Your Career." *Fast Company*, 2013.
39 Cooper, Belle Beth. (2013).
40 Hackman, G. S. and Biers, D. W. "Team Usability Testing: Are Two Heads Better Than One?" *Proceedings of the Human Factors Society Annual Meeting* 36, no. 16 (1992): 1205–1209.
41 Pendleton, David, and Furnham, Adrian. *Leadership: All You Need to Know.* New York: Palgrave Macmillan, 2011.
42 Whittington, Les. "The Authenticity Game." *The Hill Times*, October 23, 2024. https://www.hilltimes.com/story/2024/10/23/the-authenticity-game/438619/.
43 The Observer View (editorial). "Americans Who Believe in Democracy Have No Choice but to Vote for Harris." *The Guardian*, October 26, 2024.
44 Turnbull, Lori. "Leadership and the Politics of Authenticity." *Policy Options*, February 28, 2023.
45 "Transformational Leadership." Wikipedia, last modified October 2023.
46 Pendleton, David and Furnham, Adrian. (2011).

47   Bono, Joyce E. and Judge, Timothy A. "Personality and Transformational and Transactional Leadership: A Meta-Analysis." *Journal of Applied Psychology* 89, no. 5 (2004): 901–910.

48   Zopiatis, Anastasios and Constanti, Panayiota. "Extraversion, Openness, and Conscientiousness: The Route to Transformational Leadership in the Hotel Industry." *Leadership & Organization Development Journal* 33, no. 1 (2012): 86–104. Findings suggest that transformational leadership is positively associated with extraversion, openness and conscientiousness; while in contrast, passive/avoidance leadership style is negatively associated with conscientiousness and agreeableness.

49   Reynolds, Pamela. "Extroverts, Your Colleagues Wish You Would Just Shut Up and Listen." *Harvard Business School Working Knowledge*, 2022. Extroverts tend to be bad listeners despite being socially confident. Ways to signal you are listening to your colleagues include verbally repeating or paraphrasing what's been said and interjecting with affirmations like "right" or "yes." Show engagement by laughing at jokes and maintaining appropriate silence. Nonverbally, maintain eye contact, nod, and smile during conversations. Adopt an open posture by keeping hands apart and facing the speaker directly, even mirroring their posture to further demonstrate attentiveness.

50   Flynn, Francis J., Collins, H., and Zlatev, J. "Are You Listening to Me? The Negative Link between Extraversion and Perceived Listening." *Personality and Social Psychology Bulletin* 49, no. 6 (June 2023): 837–851.

51   Duffy, Kathleen A. and Chartrand, Tanya L. (2015). *cf.* note 36.

Chapter 2

The Other Side of the Coin

The Considerable Strengths and Occasional Weaknesses of Introverted Leaders

As we discussed in the introduction, the old-school view is that most leaders are extroverts rather than introverts. Our interviews with over 750 C-suite executives, however, tell us that this is simply untrue in today's world. Old ideas die hard at times. Remember General Dempsey's saying that generals fight the battles of their youth.

Introverts live in a world built for extroverts.[1] As Cain writes, "Introverts living under the Extrovert Ideal are like women in a man's world, discounted because of a trait that goes to the core of who they are."[2] As a byproduct of our extrovert-friendly system, we perceive introversion to be something one ought to overcome—we may succeed despite our possession of this trait and never because of it. We rather consistently trust loud leaders instead of quiet ones, thanks to their charismatic yet assertive natures and the comfort these qualities bring to management.

One enjoyable post by *Introvert Dear*, an award-winning community for introverts (which we quite like) listed a set of phrases that "Scare" introverts, here are a few:

1. "Let's go around the room and introduce ourselves." **The dreaded icebreaker.** Is there anything worse? Introverts might rather face a masked figure wielding a chainsaw than endure that awkward moment.
2. "*Everyone* will be there!"
   Whether it's a party, work event, or family gathering, introverts prefer to be where the crowds *are not*. **It's not about hating people** or having **enochlophobia**—they're just wired to be more sensitive to all kinds of stimulation. For an introvert, few things are scarier than the looming threat of an **introvert hangover**.
3. "Tell me about yourself."
   Can we . . . not? When asked to reveal personal details to people they barely know, introverts might feel as uncomfortable as a kid who's eaten too much Halloween candy. Ironically, they'd probably feel more at ease discussing

DOI: 10.4324/9781003612216-3

something deeper—like how a **career** setback helped them grow as a person or the physics of time travel—than making **small talk** about what they did over the weekend.

4. "I invited some friends over. I hope that's okay!"

Friends are coming . . . to my home? My sacred space? The one place where I can truly relax and be myself? For introverts, last-minute guests mean no time to mentally prepare to be "on" which is a truly terrifying prospect. The total list is 17.[3]

Scaring introverts is a way of putting it that suggests weaknesses, but we see introverts much more positively. We strongly believe that introverts possess considerable strengths that extroverts can and should learn from. In this chapter, we will highlight those strengths while still acknowledging the occasional weaknesses of introverts. We believe that understanding the strengths and weaknesses of introverts—and of all personality types, for that matter—can help you work with, manage the people that work for you and manage upward, those who do not share your personality type. And perhaps most importantly, have better insight into your own approach to leadership and life.

In comparison to seemingly competent extroverts, people tend to view introverts as a bit too meek at times. This prevailing sentiment maintains the notion that the introverted state is an obstacle to success, with 65% of senior corporate executives labelling introversion as such in 2006.[4] In recent years, however, this sentiment has begun to change, launching a radical upsurge of appreciation for quiet leaders in the business world. The previously overlooked qualities of the underdog have become exceedingly valuable in being an excellent leader in today's world.

Personality and Chemical Components of Our Introvert

There exist several common characteristics shared by most introverts. The following list details these characteristics, in comparison with some of the most common extroverted traits discussed in Chapter 1.

Introverts	Extroverts
More reserved	Outwardly enthusiastic
Like to focus on one project	Multi-tasks
Prefers to listen than take the stage	Seeks the spotlight
Think > Speak	Thinks aloud
Write > Speak	Speaking > Writing
Cautious with decision-making	"Just do it!" approach to risks
Recharges in quiet settings	Recharges in social settings
Avoids conflict	Comfortable with conflict

Let's go through the chart and hit some of the highlights. The introvert generally thinks before speaking; they tend to carefully choose their words because they have taken time to think before they speak. Your parents most likely taught you to "think before you speak," good advice that introverts are apt to follow, extroverts not as much. Extroverts are more apt just to speak up without a great deal of thought. Although this can have a certain charm and often invokes some laughter, it tends to lack depth and suggests extroverts are not as profound as introverts.

Karl tends to approach introverts about things a bit differently. When he would like an introvert to comment on something at a meeting, he will email them or chat with them and tell them, with sufficient notice, that he would like to call on them at a meeting in a couple of days about a certain topic where they are knowledgeable. With an extrovert, he might mention it to them as they walk into a meeting since an extrovert is more willing to talk off the top of their head and will tend to be amusing, charming and get things rolling. Given the lack of research and thought, these contributions might not be all that insightful. On the other hand, by giving an introvert a couple of days' notice, they will have typically done their homework, so they are rather well prepared and have insightful things to share. But don't call on them as you walk to the meeting, this will be too stressful! Even during the meeting, Karl will tend to look at them and be asking non-verbally, are you ready to comment? They often want to hear the meeting unfold and for other people to speak up before they comment. As the chart says, they prefer to listen first, then to speak.

Introverts tend to focus on one thing at a time, whereas extroverts are more apt to have multiple balls in the air. This is more stimulating, but you might drop a ball after all! This goes back to the natural difference between introverts and extroverts—their response to stimulation. Extroverts enjoy and seek stimulation, so having more than one thing at a time going on is more appealing for them.

Extroverts don't mind the spotlight. Introverts are generally not as comfortable with all the attention on them. Again, these situations each exhibit the natural response to stimuli of each respective communication style.

Introverts tend to take a more careful approach to making decisions and particularly risks. They think it through, they take their time, they do their research, in what often is a more sensible approach. Extroverts, on the other hand, tend to jump in first, ask questions later—a Nike outlook on life, more stimulating, more exhilarating, but more likely to get in trouble, as the introverts would quietly point out.

We'll cover extrovert and introvert breaks in more detail in Chapter 3, but let's briefly touch on them. Introverts take breaks to get away from too much stimulation. Examples might include walking the dog, reading a book, going for a walk with noise-cancelling headphones, quietly listening to Mozart, etc. Ask an introvert what they do to recharge. They will give you a few examples. There are articles on introvert breaks in Chapter 3 that we will share some, however, when Karl looked for research and articles on extrovert breaks, there were none to be found! He wrote an article on the five types of extrovert breaks he takes; we will review that at length in Chapter 3. For Karl, after an hour of sitting in his office by himself writing this book, he needs to escape his office. In his case, his recharge might involve the student lounge, just a 20-second walk from his office on the 3rd floor of the Bronfman Building at McGill.

The introvert gains strength from silence, whereas the extrovert often feels that they must fill silences. Both can take either of these traits too far, but both can also serve as strengths, as we discussed earlier.

Conflict is an interesting one. Again, it gets back to stimulation, extroverts don't mind some conflict because it gets the juices flowing, it is stimulating as long as you don't have too much conflict. Introverts typically find conflict to be excessive overstimulation. Of course, conflict can be helpful in resolving continuous issues and ensuring more efficient progress at times. The level of emotion and energy inherent in conflict can be problematic for introverts, and awareness of this on the part of others can help them bring out the positive side of conflict.

Carl Jung's Introvert

While the extrovert focuses on events occurring in their external environment, the introvert places a stronger emphasis on the meaning behind why and how these events occur.[5] This can be a considerable strength, as understanding the why and how events come about can lead to genuine insights and new strategies going forward. Wise extroverts will turn to introverts to gain their insights into the whys and hows to work, lead and manage more effectively.

Generally, introverts are seen as more shy, aloof, observant, analytical, and keep to themselves. They spend energy in interactions with their external environment (such as with other people) and recharge with time alone.

Carl Jung's view of introverts identifies them as introspective: they are reflective and thoughtful, often characteristically shy; they seek to understand and master social objects in their environment, regard the unknown with distrust, and at times meet outside influences with considerable resistance.[6]

Returning to Dr. Laney's study of the PET scans of introverts and extroverts, Dr. Johnson finds that not only are the blood pathways within introverts' brains more complex and involved with internal experiences, but that introverts also have more blood flow to their brain than extroverts.[7] This finding suggests a greater and more consistent internal stimulation of the introverted brain. Thus, Jung is again correct in his theory that introverts are more internally focused than extroverts in their processing mechanisms and other brain activity.[8]

Kagan's longitudinal study identifies another link between biology and personality type that solidifies Jung's view on communication style. In *Galen's Prophecy*, Kagan commends Jung for his accuracy on the relation between high- and low-reactive adolescents to introversion and extroversion.[9] His research finds that babies who react more strongly to stimuli grow up to become introverts. Babies highly sensitive to external stimuli are, as Jung would describe, uncertain and wary of their external environment, looking to understand it better before proceeding with caution.

Whereas extroverts prefer the brain pathway associated with the neurotransmitter dopamine, introverts are found to be much more sensitive to dopamine spikes and can easily feel overstimulated by activities that increase its presence in the brain (described in the last chapter as new or thrilling experiences). Introverts use acetylcholine on their more dominant pathway. This neurotransmitter affects perceptual learning, influences the ability to sustain calm and alert behaviour, and stimulates good feelings when thinking. It plays a major role in dreaming and memory function.

Additional research demonstrates that introverts prefer their parasympathetic nervous system over the sympathetic side that extroverts tend to prefer.[10] The parasympathetic system is coined as the "rest-and-digest" response. This nervous system constricts your pupils, slows your heart rate, relaxes your muscles, increases digestion, and emphasizes inner rather than outer focus. In this state, the body is focused on storing energy rather than spending it. This fits with our experience and research with introverts and extroverts. Dr. Laney believes that this key difference in preference between introverts and extroverts forms the foundation of introverted and extroverted temperaments.[11] We tend to agree with her view.

Introverts in Our Extrovert's World

The introvert's experience has likely been challenging as a result of operating in a society organized with extroverts in mind. Despite a tenacious ability to persevere through a brash, busy work atmosphere unforgiving to reserved communication styles, introverts face, at times, some systemic disadvantages inhibiting their success. Although introverted and extroverted leaders prove to be equally effective in academic and corporate environments, introverts often face exclusionary hiring processes and self-select into supportive organizations as a result.[10] In other words, organizations are less than sensitive to introverted needs and thus at times are losing out on individuals who, according to Atamanik, are humbler and more reserved in their leadership.[12] Unfortunately, this represents a missed opportunity for these companies to diversify from having extroverted executives alone.

We should not underestimate the power of a quiet-natured individual. Introverts are excellent listeners and thorough analyzers: they are capable of reading the room, considering and incorporating all ideas into analysis, and contributing optimally to discussions.[13] They also possess almost impeccable persistence, the capacity for creativity, and the capability to focus.

Grant, Gino, and Hofman (2015) argue that introverts can be more effective leaders in dynamic and unpredictable environments—settings which, as of late, have become an increasingly familiar challenge to business leaders.[14] One could argue, as McKinsey, BCG, and Bain, some of the world's leading management consultants and thinkers, that the world is more turbulent than ten or twenty years ago. When Karl is talking with older people, he says, "The world has gone nuts!" With undergrads, he is more circumspect and says the world is more turbulent than it used to be. Regardless of word choice, this appears to be very much true. This finding is intriguing, as it contradicts previous research that suggests that extroverts alone triumph during crises.

Grant and Cain are at the forefront of a new movement supporting introverts as strong leaders of the C-suite. This chapter aims to outline the growing recognition of quiet leaders in a previously exclusionary environment as well as the soft and interpretive introverts' strengths, shortcomings, and potential opportunities for them to improve.

Strength #1: The Underestimated Power of Listening

I love to listen to people. I love to learn by listening. I would rather listen to other people.

Daniel Lamarre (Executive Vice Chairman and former CEO of
Cirque du Soleil)

Perhaps the most pronounced strength of the introvert is the ability to listen when someone else is speaking. Marissa West, CEO of General Motors Canada, believes that "Learning to listen more than you speak is an art of leadership."

One of the most powerful qualities of introverted leaders is their ability to listen. In a fast-paced world where people are quick to speak and slow to hear, introverts bring a refreshing change. They aren't preoccupied with dominating conversations or proving themselves through words; instead, they focus on absorbing information, understanding different viewpoints, and making well-considered decisions.

Introverts are much more likely than extroverts to hear and internalize what others are saying. This skill allows the introvert to gain potentially valuable information from interactions that, although available to everyone in the conversation, are only utilized by those who really listen. The best leaders are those who actually hear what others are saying. This ability to listen is especially valuable in leadership because it fosters trust. Employees feel heard and valued when their leader truly listens to their feedback, concerns and ideas.

As British leadership professor Benjamin Laker puts it so well,

Introverted leaders are often seen as more approachable and empathetic because they create a space where team members feel comfortable expressing themselves. This listening-driven leadership style also enhances team performance. When people feel listened to, they are more likely to contribute their best ideas and work collaboratively. Introverted leaders, by focusing on collective input rather than personal dominance, help teams thrive by ensuring that all voices are heard.[15]

In an extreme scenario, a room full of extroverts might mean everyone is speaking and no one is listening. Everyone launches their ideas into the discussion, but nothing is picked up by other contributors or authentically built upon. This exercise will likely prove to be a waste of time. Nobel argues that an extrovert leading a team of extroverts is a liability.[16] The team will be unable to collaborate or build on ideas, as the leader is behaving like their followers: nobody is collecting and integrating everyone's loose thoughts.

Given that extroverts have ascended the corporate ladder more often than introverts as a consequence of the culture of personality, conference rooms full of executives deliberating in this manner are not abnormal. In this circumstance, the introverted leader can step in, listen to the ideas of extroverted participants, and integrate these streams of thought into something valuable.

We know—this strength seems basic, perhaps too elementary to be referenced in an academic book. However, living in a culture of personality has made true listeners scarce, and good listening an extraordinary trait. The introvert often acquires excess information from her listening ear, some of which she may put to good use. Introverted leaders' greater listening skills and receptivity to suggestions make them promising leaders, especially in the presence of loud subordinates.

In a study conducted on introverted and extroverted pizza delivery managers, Grant et al. concluded that because introverted managers were more open-minded to employee ideas on increasing the efficiency of operations, their franchises earned 16% higher profits than average (while franchises run by extrovert managers earned 14% lower profits than average).[17] In another study with similar objectives, Grant et al. found introverted leaders to promote a higher productivity rate—28% above average.

Penny Wise, President and Managing Director of 3M, believes introverts have a special skill:

> My introversion helps me be a good listener and helps me to join together lots of different opinions to figure out a solution. . . . There is a nugget in there that you need to listen to because it will inform a better outcome.

3M is a company for introverts. Known for its policy encouraging solo research and experimentation, the company has encouraged its workforce to dedicate 15% of their hours on exploratory projects and creative inventions of their choosing since the mid-20th century. In addition to being an introvert's dream, this policy has been remarkably fruitful. It birthed their Cubitron sanding film discs, the AEX Hybrid Purifier, and even Post-It Notes. It is likely one of the reasons the company is so large today.

Strength #2: Readers of the Room, Less is More

> You know, I think introverts listen. I think they observe better. When they speak, they tend to be a little bit more measured.
>
> Paul Desmarais III (Chairman and CEO at Sagard Holdings)

Extroverts work the room, but introverts read the room. While the extrovert speaks, the introvert observes and, by association, learns. Dan Bilefesky, international correspondent for the *New York Times*, believes, "If you don't say much, then your source might fill in the gap of silence."

In this case, by source we refer to coworkers, but the same meaning applies.

As they actively observe their environment, introverts are granted the opportunity to notice more than simply what they hear. Introverts could, for instance, read body language that cues them into the underlying dynamics of a team—the unspoken signals at every meeting.

What is the implication of such greater awareness? The introvert will notice those who have been silent. They are in a position to learn from those who have not spoken, in addition to those who have. Similar to the result of their authentic listening skills, this ability may pick up details or insights unavailable to an extrovert focused on contribution rather than perception. They understand the room better. This asset has the potential to change the final decision in an important way.

Yale psychologists Gollwitzer and Bargh conducted a study on assessing the predictions of social behaviour in group settings.[18] They asked 1100 participants questions about how others would behave in specific circumstances. Their results show introverts as more intuitively apt at judging how others feel, think, and behave in given social scenarios. Gollwitzer believes the results are explainable given the introvert's detached, outsider perspective from the social environment: "Introverts [are] looking out at the world . . . they may more accurately judge how most people are behaving or acting or feeling."[19]

The extroverted personality is often considered as the better communicator and relationship builder. However, a large and thundering presence is not always needed to impress powerful people. The introvert, unlike the extrovert, is engrossed introspectively and does not feel the need to consistently engage with their environment. During team meetings, the extrovert's engagement likely takes the form of contributions to the discussion, often leading to domination. As alluded to previously, there is a risk of reduced listening and an internalization of others' views if domination is a factor.

Conversely, the introvert never dominates a discussion and only contributes if necessary—usually meaning when they share thoughts, the whole room is eager to hear them, knowing that they are about to say something insightful and transformative. "When you speak, people take it as truth . . . everybody listens," asserts Dr. Joanne Liu, former international president of Doctors Without Borders.

If they speak rarely, the few verbal contributions made by introverts are bound to be worthwhile. What the introvert says is usually more valuable, according to Mitch Garber (lawyer, investor, business executive, member of the Order of Canada, board member of Rackspace, NHL Seattle, etc.): "I have worked with very cerebral leaders who speak very little and when they do speak, it is more meaningful than when I speak."

Strength #3: Refined Internal Processing Mechanisms

> Introverts tend to think a little bit longer and they're not quite as, you know, ready, shoot, aim as some of the rest of us.
>
> Linda Hasenfratz (CEO at Linamar Corporation)

Introverts think more than extroverts. In 2012, the *Journal of Neuroscience* published a study demonstrating that introverts have thicker grey matter in their prefrontal cortex, an area of the brain for abstract thought and decision-making.[20] As mentioned earlier, Johnson found greater blood flow patterns in the brain pathways of introverts and a stronger devotion to internal processing.[21] These findings suggest that introverts expend greater brain power on thinking rather than acting, and solidifies our findings in this chapter and the one prior: introverts think to talk whereas extroverts think aloud.

When this well-practiced thinking is combined with a capacity to listen carefully and read the room, the introvert comes to hone strong internal processing mechanisms. Before expressing a view, introverts hear all other opinions, internalize them, process them, and consider them in the development of their own viewpoint. This process might result in more balanced decision-making, especially because it all occurs internally and without the influence of others in their environment. Extroverts' decision-making occurs out loud and is therefore a more spontaneous strategy. They are often influenced easily by the majority opinion while processing their thoughts, regardless of this opinion's accuracy.[22]

Brad Martin, former president and CEO of Penguin Random House, appreciates the introverted capacity of reflection: "I am known for making quick decisions, but I think people do not see the thought I put in before it happens. Because of this, I suspect most of my colleagues would not consider me an introvert."

In her experience with introverts, Heather Chalmers has also noticed parallel qualities,

> They take the time to really think things through before they speak, so when they do speak, they've considered different points of view already. And so I always find when you get that sort of opinion or comment, I make a real point of listening to it because it's been very, very well-thought-out.

As the subheading quote, from our interview with Linda Hasenfratz, outlines, most extroverts think on their feet and thus solve problems and execute solutions aloud and quickly. Introverts, on the other hand, take the time to reflect using their internal processing mechanisms before a finalized decision is made. Both approaches have their advantages, depending on the circumstances and the task at hand. Obviously, sometimes we might prefer leaders who take the time to consider all factors to decide in a crisis—those who, as Kat Tchernavskikh, two-time entrepreneur and *Forbes* 30 Under 30 recipient, "take in the entire environment for processing, not immediately reacting."

We should note a positive side effect of the introvert's internalized process— generally, the moral compass of the introvert can be superior to that of the extrovert.[23] Introverts are less drawn to influences outside of themselves, and so when making ethical decisions or facing a moral challenge, they will process this problem with criteria that remain similar, and thus the results they produce are consistent. Of course, this conclusion depends on the necessary assumption that the introvert in question is a relatively moral person—an introvert with backward morals would obviously be less ethical than a moral extrovert.

Strength #4: Greater Focus, Creativity, and Passion

> I found that many of my fellow speakers on the lecture circuit are introverts because they are very often the people who are committed deeply to a particular topic.
>
> Susan Cain (Author)

It is more common for the introvert to remain focused, persistent, and creative over an extended period. Extroverts often require a dynamic and diverse external environment to entertain them. It is difficult for them to sit down alone and concentrate on one project for too long—because they will be engaging only with themselves, they are more apt to become bored. Introverts, however, thrive in this setting. They enjoy themselves when alone and can therefore sit for hours working on certain tasks or projects. Here, they learn the strength of focus and persistence.

Another outcome of this time spent is mastery. One prominent neuroscience researcher and author, Frederike Fabritius, suggested that 70% of gifted people are introverts because they are the ones who enjoy spending time alone, avoiding distraction, and dedicating hours to focusing on their craft.[24] Albert Einstein, for example, claimed his excellence did not come from innate intelligence. Instead, his ability to sit down for hours and focus on problems allowed him to appreciate and understand subjects until they became his passions.[25] This can be challenging for many extroverts, but can be learned to at least some degree.

If the introvert can become specialized in and master a subject, they then have the potential to perform very well in jobs that require specific expertise. If they have the dedication to master several subjects, they become well-rounded managers, as they know the ins and outs of their areas and can make comprehensive decisions. Their promotions, therefore, tend to occur based on knowledge and merit, instead of personal connection and networking (as might be more common for extroverts), making them well-respected C-suite executives.

Introverts tend to enjoy socializing and public speaking much less in comparison with extroverts, who are comfortable engaging a crowd. However, one caveat to this generality involves passion projects. Indeed, according to Susan Cain, "you talk to thousands of people, but as an introvert, what allows you to? It is because of the topic; it allows you to do that in a comfortable way."[26] When someone is committed deeply to a particular subject, introvert or extrovert, they can share their passion with others, even if this involves public speaking. When they do speak about their passions, the words flow out of them effortlessly and eloquently, as they should, given the long hours of time dedicated to thinking about the subject.

Scott Crowder, Vice President at IBM Quantum, resonates with this experience:

> I am never going to be the person who builds relationships at a cocktail party. But I am quite comfortable going in cold to talk about cloud computing at the front of a room with lots of people because I am passionate about that. I am also more succinct in my words because I do not like to talk.

Networking for Introverts

Let's start off with advice from Keith Ferrazzi, *New York Times* best-selling author of *Never Eat Alone*. This is a great book that Karl recommends to his students.

"I'm not a good networker because I'm an introvert." If you've ever thought this, you're not alone. It's easy to assume that extraversion and charisma are the key to building a great network. But it's a myth.

"Great networking isn't about being the loudest person in the room or having the perfect icebreaker. It's about building authentic, meaningful relationships in a way that feels natural to you." Keith goes on to argue that,

> In fact, introverts often make the best networkers. They focus on deep, genuine connections rather than surface-level interactions. They are great listeners,

which builds trust quickly. And they bring thoughtfulness and intentionality to every relationship.

Here is Keith's advice,

first things first; Lead with authenticity and with generosity. For me, it takes less energy to lead and walk into a room or a meeting with heart than by trying to fake being the energetic, outgoing person that makes their way around the room, chatting with everybody. It takes less energy to walk into a room and really be curious truly, and get to know people truly.

And I just find that the more authentic I am about being of service and developing real relationships, even as an introvert, the more I thrive.

We believe this is also great advice for extroverts and the way they should network as well.

Introverts network a bit differently, but their approach can be very powerful, and a real connection with people is what extroverts, indeed everyone, should strive towards. Our experience is that too many introverts unnecessarily shy away from using their strengths for better networking. Depending on what profession, industry, etc., you are in, networking is helpful. But in a more turbulent business world, we believe networking is an important skill. From the viewpoint of enjoying the neighbourhood you live in and the place you work, networking is also a helpful skill. Practice, practice, practice is helpful.

Shortcomings of the Introvert

I am not a natural leader. Some people are born to lead naturally. I was probably too introverted, too in my bubble head.

Louis Vachon (CEO of National Bank)

Although introverts possess a plethora of invaluable traits that, in the business world, are relatively uncommon, they can also exhibit some qualities that do not serve them well. Of course, this is inevitable, given that they are frequently required to act out of character to meet the extroverted requirements of leadership positions.

Weakness #1: Overthinking

The danger of an introvert is paralysis by analysis. They overthink and then they never contribute.

Karl Moore, borrowing Paul Sislian's phrase in an interview . . .

Introverts' reliance on their own thoughts and internal processes puts them at considerable risk of overthinking, a pattern also evident in a biological context. According to Dr. Laurie Helgoe, brain scans of introverts, even ones at rest, consistently show more activity than those of extroverts. Because introverts are always thinking, it follows logically that they may at times dwell too much on a topic.[27]

Dr. Laney's theories on how introverts process stimuli differently from extroverts might also explain the introvert's overthinking tendencies.[28] Stimuli entering the introverted brain travel a longer pathway, including the right front insular (self-reflection, emotional meaning, error identification), Broca's area (speech, self-talk), right and left frontal lobes (evaluation, thought processing, decisions), and the left hippocampus (categorizes memories). The introvert prefers to process information more thoroughly.

Although overthinking is by definition a weakness in itself (otherwise we would call it thinking), the danger is that consistently exhibiting such behaviour might cause hesitation to take charge, make decisions, or take action appropriately—role requirements that are essential factors of effective leadership. Though to be honest, in the world of 2025, hesitating before making a big, dramatic decision is seen a bit more positively than in the past. We live in a more turbulent, uncertain world. Some hesitation to apply yesterday's solutions today is not necessarily a bad thing! The executive often faces decisions of high time sensitivity or scenarios that require immediate action, such as strategic interactions with competition, the discovery of a new consumer trend, or the pending release of poor quarterly reports or problematic company scandals. In such situations, the confidence and certainty of action common among extroverts are valuable traits to ensure that the firm does not lose out as a consequence of unnecessarily postponing a decision. Such advantages of the extrovert explain why, in most research, extroverts are known to be trusted leaders in times of crisis.

Weakness #2: Social Anxiety and Lack of Assertiveness

> Leading is like a big encounter with yourself to a certain extent because this is the time that you feel the most vulnerable and the most, I would say, on your own . . . All of a sudden there are thousands of eyes watching you. . . . Since I'm much more of an introvert, it required me to work on myself.
> —Dr. Joanne Liu (former international president of Doctors Without Borders)

In addition to team management, leaders of major groups or corporations or other organizations must be able to present a public image. A major part of the executive role involves public speaking and networking to strategically promote the company and create opportunities for further development. Naturally, this leader will spend significant time engaging with their external environment and exchanging energies with others. For large publicly traded companies, this means that senior executives, particularly the CEO, must spend considerable amounts of time selling their organization to encourage investors to buy shares in the company, analysts that follow their company/industry to recommend their stock, large investors to keep their investments in the firm, or press to write positive articles about the future of the company.

Karl has had a number of CEOs and other senior executives come to class. For larger organizations that have thousands of employees around the world, the CEO often spends more time selling the new strategy than coming up with the strategy. They often use the analogy of a rowing team, where the team must row together, their paddles moving at the same time in the same direction, otherwise the boat will veer off in one direction or another. That is why a small man or woman with a big voice sits in the back of the boat, not rowing but making sure that by yelling out a stroke in a loud voice that they keep the team rowing together in the same direction. The CEO, CFO, COO's, etc., job is to make sure thousands of employees understand the new strategy and are working to go in the same direction to deliver the desired result of the new approach. Some introverts find that having to deliver a message across an organization consistently and repeatedly is the most draining and anxiety-inducing part of leadership.

Bèla Fleck, perhaps the top jazz banjo player in the world, told us that he is an introverted musician and faces this problem constantly:

> I would not perform if I didn't have to in order to be a musician. I rarely speak on stage, and I have learned to speak as little as possible. I tend to perform with people who are my equal or better; I like to work with people I do not have to manage. I just don't enjoy controlling people.

From Bèla's viewpoint, it is controlling, but from a more extroverted viewpoint, it is about working effectively together and getting a bigger result because of our shared efforts versus more individual efforts. Which Bèla does but in a quieter way.

Introverts might not enjoy dealing with the public, in part due to social anxiety and in part due to the requirement that they must assert themselves towards others. Whereas the extrovert can be perceived as too assertive, even aggressive, the introvert is usually seen as not assertive enough. This is understandable, as it is widely accepted that an assertive individual is more likely to be extroverted. Indeed, according to the Big Five personality traits, also known as the Five Factor Model (FFM), assertiveness is one of the two dimensions used to assess extraversion.[29] Chapter 4 will further explore the two dimensions of the personality trait extraversion-introversion, its strengths, and its weaknesses according to the FFM. For the moment, let's keep in mind that assertiveness is a key trait of extraversion and that this connection highlights one of the main difficulties introverted leaders face.

Being less practiced at engaging with their external environment than extroverts, the introvert is not as likely to speak up, take control when necessary, or, most importantly, lead in difficult environments. In the event where a team needs a loud persona to quickly and efficiently guide them to success, extroverts may be better equipped for the task. Employees may also require constant advice and guidance, which might be exhausting for an introvert to provide. Introverted leaders can quickly lose respect from subordinates if they do not engage with their employees and assert themselves to the same extent as their extroverted counterparts.

Whereas introverts might have this ability in the case of passion projects or areas of their expertise, they require environments where they can comfortably engage themselves in their work in order to provide for others. Top-level C-suite executive positions tend to be much more generalist, concerned with overall strategy rather than connecting details, as with specific skill roles or passion projects. Extroverts, even if generalist in their skill set, are more capable of being assertive and engaging a team regardless of the team's subject of involvement.

Just as an extrovert leading a group of extroverts is more apt to be unproductive, a team built solely of introverts is usually problematic. This version of unproductivity takes the form of over-contemplation and a lack of discussion. Nobel argues that passive followers benefit from an extroverted leader who can encourage discussion and promote a welcoming organizational culture where employees become comfortable speaking up and sharing.[30]

Our Key Takeaways

#1 Introverts' abilities are highly complementary to one another.

Introverts can encourage contributions from subordinates and interpret and incorporate multiple opinions into one. This is an asset. Paired with their capability for internal analysis and decision-making, introverts can formulate and evaluate comprehensive and meticulous strategies and then share this well-developed plan with their team. They are a one-stop shop for idea integration, development, refinement, and finalization. The product of this process is consistently high-quality and trustworthy.

#2 Introverts often have a steeper learning curve than extroverts, but this pays off in the long run.

Operating in a world built for the opposite communication style, the introvert has had to make vast strides to fit into the requirements of the current system. They have been forced to act out of character to survive this extrovert-oriented system. Significant efforts have been made by introverts to learn effective leadership skills that come naturally to extroverted individuals, something that has likely been an uncomfortable experience. However, the nature of the skills they have had to learn is such that they can be easily and explicitly practiced. Public speaking, making conversation, and improving sociability, for example, are skills that can be trained aloud repetitively until proficient. The same cannot be said for an extrovert trying to direct focus internally and become more introverted, as these processes have been known to be difficult to replicate reliably. Once the introvert's new skills are mastered, introverted executives will become well-rounded and adaptable to leadership in any situation—particularly because they will retain their own unique skills in addition to these common executive traits.

#3 Introverts can be taken as more inspiring leaders.

Because they are apt to listen and think before they jump in, many people find this more inspiring than the extroverted leaders who are more apt to jump when others are expressing their thoughts. This can be very well received indeed. And in a more turbulent, more uncertain world, this can mean getting more up-to-date ideas, strategies and approaches—with big potential payoffs.

Notes

1 Stephens-Craig, Dana, Kuofie, Matthew, and Dool, Richard. "Perception of Introverted Leaders by Mid to High-Level Leaders." *Journal of Marketing and Management* 6, no. 1 (2015): 62–75. Investigates the interplay of introversion and extroversion in leadership. Through investigation of mid to high-level leaders' perception of introversion, the study aims to connect positive traits of introverts to desirable leadership roles. The research emphasizes the need to recognize and value the contributions of introverted leaders, challenging traditional biases in favor of extroverted leadership traits in the workplace.
2 Cain, Susan. *Quiet: The Power of Introverts in a World That Can't Stop Talking*. New York: Crown Publishing Group, 2012.
3 Granneman, Jenn. "Introverts' Scariest Phrases." *IntrovertDear,* October 30, 2024. https://introvertdear.com/news/introverts-scariest-phrases/.
4 Stephens-Craig, Dana, Kuofie, Matthew, and Dool, Richard. (2015).
5 Jung, Carl Gustav. (1923). Emphasized the necessity of mutual psychological understanding when these two types interact, whether in personal relationships or professional settings. Translating this to the modern context, the paper argues that society has predominantly tailored itself to extroverted norms, often compelling introverts to adapt to an extroverted worldview. This forced adaptation can lead to internal conflict and may hinder introverts from realizing their full potential. Instead of pressuring introverted leaders to conform to extroverted stereotypes, the paper advocates for recognizing and nurturing the unique strengths and potential of introverts in the workplace.
6 Jung, Carl Gustav. (1923).

7   Laney, Marti Olsen. *The Introvert Advantage: How Quiet People Can Thrive in an Extrovert World.* New York: Workman Publishing Company, 2002. Dr. Marti Olsen Laney explores the strengths and challenges of introverts, debunking common misconceptions. The book provides insights and strategies for introverts to navigate an extroverted world, emphasizing the value of their unique abilities in various life aspects.

8   Cain, Susan. (2012).

9   Cain, Susan. (2012).

10 Cain, Susan and Granneman, Jennifer. "Why Introverts and Extroverts are Different: The Science." *Quiet Schools Network* (2016): 1. https://www.quietrev.com/wp-content/uploads/2016/05/Why-Introverts-and-Extroverts-Are-Different-The-Science-by-Jennifer-Grannerman.pdf.

11 Laney, Marti Olsen. (2002): 76.

12 Atamanik, Candace. "The Introverted Leader: Examining the Role of Personality and Environment." *Center for Leadership Current Research* 2 (2013): 10. https://digitalcommons.fiu.edu/lead_research/2.

13 Stephens-Craig, Dana, Kuofie, Matthew, and Dool, Richard. (2015): 62–75.

14 Grant, Adam, Gino, Francesca, and Hofmann, David A. "The Hidden Advantages of Quiet Bosses." *Harvard Business Review*, 2015.

15 This paragraph owes much to Laker, Ben. "The Quiet, Transformative Power of Introverted Leaders." *Forbes.com,* October 14, 2024. We do recommend his thinking.

16 Nobel, Carmen. "Introverts: The Best Leaders for Proactive Employees." *Harvard Business School,* 2010.

17 Grant, Adam, Gino, Francesca, and Hofmann, David A. (2015).

18 https://econtent.hogrefe.com/doi/full/10.1027/1864-9335/a000332.

19 Leibowitz, Gwen. "Yale Psychologists: Introverts Are Better Than Extroverts at Performing This Essential Leadership Skill." *Inc.*, 2018.

20 Holmes, Avram J., et al. "Individual Differences in Amygdala-Medial Prefrontal Anatomy Link Negative Affect, Impaired Social Functioning, and Polygenic Depression Risk." *The Journal of Neuroscience* 32, no. 50 (2012): 18087–18100. https://doi.org/10.1523/jneurosci.2531–12.2012.

21 Laney, Marti Olsen. (2002): 76.

22 Tuovinen, Sanna, Tang, Xin, and Salmela-Aro, Katariina. "Introversion and Social Engagement: Scale Validation, Their Interaction, and Positive Association with Self-Esteem." *Frontiers in Psychology* 11 (2020). https://doi.org/10.3389/fpsyg.2020.590748.

23 "People who are strong introverts (I) tend to be more self-reflective and self-reliant in decision-making. This is opposed to extroverts (E) who may be more reactive in their decision-making" Binkley, J. K. and Baggs T. W. "Influence of Personality on Ethical Decision-Making in Communication Sciences and Disorders." *The Internet Journal of Allied Health Sciences and Practice* 22, no. 1 (2023): Article 17.

24 Fabritius, Friederike. "A Neuroscientist Shares the 4 'Highly Coveted' Skills that Set Introverts Apart: 'Their Brains Work Differently.'" *CNBC* (2023). https://www.cnbc.com/2023/02/07/neuroscientist-shares-coveted-skills-that-set-introverts-apart-their-brains-work-differently.html.

25 "Albert Einstein Quotes." *BrainyQuote.com.* BrainyMedia Inc., 2023.

26 Moore, Karl and Cain, Susan. "The CEO Series with McGill's Karl Moore: Susan Cain, New York Times Bestselling Author and Speaker." *iHeartRadio Podcasts*, 2023.

27 Helgoe, Laurie. *Introvert Power: Why Your Inner Life Is Your Hidden Strength.* Naperville: Sourcebooks, 2008.

28 Laney, Marti Olsen. (2002).
29 John, Oliver P. and Srivastava, Sanjay. "The Big Five Trait Taxonomy: History, Measurement, and Theoretical Perspectives." In *Handbook of Personality: Theory and Research*, edited by Lawrence A. Pervin and Oliver P. John, 102–138. 2nd ed. New York: Guilford Press, 1999.
30 Nobel, Carmen. (2010).

Chapter 3

Why Striking a Balance is the Best Approach

I am still more introverted than extroverted, but I am more balanced than I have ever been.

Denis Ricard (President and CEO at Industrial Alliance, a financial firm with over 9,600 employees)

Denis Ricard is the CEO of one of Canada's largest wealth management groups. As the leader of a publicly listed company, Denis is under constant scrutiny and must balance his natural introversion with the extroverted demands of his role. His remarkable 97% CEO approval rating in 2022 is due in part (at least we believe) to his success in achieving this balance.

Flexibility on the Introvert-Extrovert Continuum

Introversion and extroversion are not definitive terms where we are all the time one or the other, for most of us—they are fluid. The extreme versions of these labels make up the boundaries of a bell curve, which resembles a random distribution of personalities spread across the bell curve. It is possible to be more extroverted than a fellow extrovert, and less introverted than other introverts. Karl, for example, is one of the biggest social butterflies in his faculty at McGill. Many extroverts are less gregarious and noisy than he is—anyone who has met him will tend to agree.

However, as is often the case with spectrums, there are substantial advantages to occupying the moderate position. Whereas the poles are located far from one another and lack similarities or common ground, central positions allow for greater ambiguity between the two sides and, subsequently, greater practice with the qualities of both extremes. There is something to be said for balance, because it leads to more adept flexibility across leadership and communication styles.

Flexibility has become a vital trait for success in our rapidly evolving and unpredictable corporate world.[1] Recent times of uncertainty and turbulence have confirmed that resilient adaptability is an important prerequisite for effective

DOI: 10.4324/9781003612216-4

leadership. Regardless of their position on the introvert-extrovert spectrum, virtually all of the executives we interviewed seem to exhibit two key commonalities: situational awareness and the capacity to balance their introverted and extroverted qualities to achieve the very needed flexibility.

In other words, these CEOs have developed the capability to identify when the need for flexibility is present, as well as the tools to fill this need.

We believe that better executives/leaders and professionals have mastered the art of self and situational awareness. They are highly skilled at evaluating their external environment and fine-tuning their behaviour accordingly to lead their team, work with key customers, the board, etc. As we may recall, introverts are particularly proficient at observing their surroundings. Regardless of their personal introversion or extroversion, all executives must be vigilant of social cues from their employees, customers, and competitors, and must adjust their leadership approach to the situations they face with a consideration of these influential factors.

According to Anthony Tjan, CEO of Cue Ball and *New York Times* best-selling author, self-awareness trumps all else as the most important quality among successful entrepreneurs, managers, and leaders.[2] It allows them to understand their strengths and weaknesses, balance conviction with humility, and remain open-minded to embracing opposing opinions.[3] Although such processes are simple in theory, they can be challenging and at times tiresome in practice—especially if it is a new idea to a person. They are mastered only with significant practical exposure to observing diverse personalities across a wide range of projects.

During our interviews, executives also expressed an appreciation for the transformative journeys they have undergone in order to become more flexible individuals. Their conscious efforts to observe the social dynamics of their surroundings led to an increased understanding of better leadership responses. However, the senior status these individuals have reached in their respective fields means that they can achieve more than the recognition of ideal conduct alone—these CEOs are capable of adopting behaviours and traits suitable to the circumstances at hand and driving organizational results. This skill is a bit of an extraordinary one, given that required behaviours often run counter at times to the natural tendencies of the executive leader. Even extroverts and introverts on respective ends of the spectrum can make continuous efforts to expand their comfort zone and, when necessary, exhibit qualities that they do not naturally possess.

Free Trait Theory

The concept that people can, at times, act out of character to advance their interests is not a new one. In his works on Free Trait Theory, the eminent professor of psychology and researcher Brian Little has developed this idea at length. In his

2008 study called *Personal Projects and Free Traits: Personality and Motivation Reconsidered*, he argues that quality of life is contingent upon the sustainable pursuit of personal projects, a mechanism that often requires the strategic substitution of biogenic fixed traits for culturally scripted behaviours.[4] In other words, our well-being depends on core projects where we can act in a role that contradicts our inherent inclinations (extroversion or introversion) to achieve our goals.

We found three takeaways from Brian Little's study:

We Can Behave Differently from Our Biogenic Fixed Traits (Free Traits Theory)

"Free traits are culturally scripted patterns of conduct that are strategically crafted to advance projects about which a person cares deeply. Biogenic introverts, for example, may act as extroverts in order to advance projects requiring expressions of enthusiastic assertiveness."[5]

According to Little, we are born with fixed traits that significantly influence our personality and remain relatively constant throughout our lives. However, our general satisfaction is dependent upon accomplishments that might require the conscious substitution of these inherited traits for what Little calls *free traits*, which offer a greater likelihood to advance important personal endeavours. His work suggests quite clearly that individuals can act contrary to their natural inclinations when the situation demands it. We are more adaptive than we believe: this means that despite our apprehension about behaving in ways that oppose our natural tendencies, we are capable of doing so in order to accomplish a project. It implies that the willingness to achieve a goal may be stronger than the fear related to the process. This provides an initial example of flexibility in personality traits, particularly in the introversion-extroversion spectrum. To become effective leaders, executives must cultivate the ability to behave in ways that occasionally contradict their inherent inclinations.

By acting out of character, they will foster new competencies that may not have been explored otherwise, a valuable asset that will lead them to success. As time goes by, people become more comfortable with the new way of acting, get better at it and over time can make it part of their repertoire. They will not only foster new competencies but also achieve goals that they could not have reached if they had not put themselves outside of their comfort zones. Our research supports this idea and shows that most executives exhibit behaviours very much in accordance with Free Trait Theory.

The Significant Cost of Free Traits

We understand that the adoption of free traits creates benefits, but it can also have a cost. Indeed, according to Brian Little, "free traits may enhance life quality by promoting core projects, but protracted free-traited behavior may compromise emotional and physical health."[6] In his study, Little uses the example of Elisabeth to illustrate this point.

Elisabeth is an introvert who has learned to behave as the extrovert of the office to please clients. Because of the needs of her company and her personal objectives, she has taken more and more responsibility to become the principal contact for social engagement and community matters. Everybody believes that she is extroverted, and her firm greatly benefits from her efforts. However, handling such socially demanding requirements has taken a toll on her. She loses herself in this role, and her anxiety has risen so high that she has to be hospitalized. Karl has run into more than a few people who have taken on roles that are too much of a mismatch with their personalities, as Elisabeth did. Thankfully, most came to see it and moved on to other roles that more fit with their personality and did not experience the extreme toll that Elisabeth experienced. Flexibility is one thing, pushing it too far is another.

In today's competitive workplace, the adaptive demands placed on individuals often requires them to act contrary to their innate traits. This can lead at times, as we see in her story, to significant mental and emotional exhaustion that could go as far as causing burnout. Are there mitigators or solutions that could prevent managers from ending up in this kind of situation?

This brings us to the final takeaway:

Mitigators

Little explains that "the costs of free-traited behavior can be mitigated by the provision and use of restorative resources."[7] For someone using free traits to achieve an objective, "a diversity of restorative resources can be used, including restorative states such as meditation for overloaded introverts."[8] This strategy will be developed in the following chapters as "extroverted and introverted breaks." The importance of those breaks in the everyday routines of executives and how it helped them become more effective leaders will be discussed in the following chapters.

However, Little also advocates for a "need for greater awareness and sharing of information between individuals about the extent to which they are engaging in free trait action." Elisabeth believed she was more extroverted and did not realize that she needed more introverted breaks, such as solitary time, to recharge. If she had had a better understanding of her biogenic traits, she could have communicated to her colleagues that she needed more time in her comfort zone because she was struggling with the numerous interpersonal projects. She might have also found someone more extroverted to handle those tasks. This understanding is an important insight for every company, as delegating tasks can be an effective solution when leaders are overusing their free traits.

In conclusion, business executives should learn greater situational awareness and the capacity to *strike a balance* in order to advance their interests related to personal development, corporate success, or some combination of the two. As a form of Little's "core personal project," such a process awakens a greater flexibility of behaviour that enables these individuals' success in their respective project goals and simultaneously promotes their ascension up the corporate ladder. Nevertheless, playing a role may take a toll and worsen one's quality of life. By having restorative niches and having a greater self-awareness, the executive's use of free traits will become more sustainable, making them more capable of operating at their best, ultimately putting their career and company on a more successful path.

Growth Versus Fixed Mindset

Is it possible to remain fluid across the continuum and strike this balance constantly, especially if walking the line is a foreign concept? With the appropriate mindset, absolutely—but it's not just about adapting in the moment. While the free traits theory emphasizes context and goal-oriented flexibility, the growth mindset offers a long-term approach that reshapes our abilities and perspectives over time.

Famed Stanford psychology professor Carol Dweck popularized this idea of a growth mindset, which involves the belief that one's abilities can change and that one may develop new skills throughout their lifetime. A fixed mindset, in contrast, prefers the belief that one is born with the talents and skills they will use in all their endeavours. For example, those with a fixed mindset view assessments as an opportunity to measure their intelligence level against others. Those with a growth mindset, on the other hand, view these assessments as opportunities to identify and understand what they do not know.

In Dweck's research, those with growth mindsets proved more likely to accept difficult challenges and put in extra time and effort, leading to skill development and higher achievement.[9] Put simply, these individuals do not feel limited by their own knowledge, viewing it instead as a reservoir that will grow as they err and learn. To develop a growth mindset, Dweck recommends emphasizing the process and learning curve rather than the end result and embracing failure as an opportunity to learn rather than seeing it as a sign of inadequacy.

Corporate individuals with a growth mindset will emphasize taking risks to gather knowledge and learn from their mistakes. They are more likely to place themselves in environments where they can learn opposite communication styles and will thus become well-versed in the practice of both introvert and extrovert archetypes. Soon enough, they will have no problem walking the line and striking a continuous balance between introversion and extroversion as is required of them in their daily tasks, making them better leaders and valuable assets to their company.

Tailoring Behaviour . . .

Due to the nature of their position, CEOs must become increasingly aware and flexible in order to meet external and internal expectations for themselves, thereby promoting the advancement of a particular goal or strategy for their company's or their own prosperity. As they expose themselves to diverse circumstances, their growth mindset will allow them to learn and master the flexibility and awareness needed to succeed in their role as managers. Let us direct our attention to three dimensions in which this process occurs:

. . . Tailoring Behaviour to the Task at Hand

> Around my friends, I am wild. But if I was in politics running for mayor and in a room with 100 people, I would talk to a few and then go home. Depending on the context, I am an introvert or extrovert.
>
> Balarama Holness (Politician, former Canadian football player in the Canadian Football League, which won the Canadian Grey Cup)

All situations are uniquely complex; therefore, the optimal response must be tailored to the problem and formulated with a consideration of group dynamics between stakeholders. Diverse objectives require different approaches to the task. Extroverted behaviours might be ideal under certain circumstances and counterproductive in others, and the same can be said for introverted behaviours. The successful executive will know when to change their behaviour to best suit the task at hand. According to Mark Hantho, Vice Chairman, Banking, Capital Markets, and Advisory at Citigroup Inc., "You can choose where you want to be in that continuum, depending on the circumstances."

The previous chapters have discussed typical strengths and shortcomings of introverts and extroverts. Here, we will outline the different steps of common ways for more senior managers that demonstrate the benefits of navigating between the strengths of each communication style when appropriate and always keeping in mind your need to be authentic, to a degree, to your natural introverted, ambiverted or extroverted nature.

When delivering a public speech, managers must appear calm, collected, and confident **(extrovert)**.

They must engage the audience through their eloquence and passion in order to further the company's objectives with greater brand awareness, customer loyalty, and strong leader representation **(extrovert)**.

They prepared a well-thought-out script **(introvert)** and know how and when to go ad-lib if the moment is right **(extrovert)**.

At the post-presentation networking cocktail, managers schmooze business partners and prospective clientele with their charisma **(extrovert)**. He listens to their take **(introvert)** and reassures their concerns **(extrovert)**.

The next morning at a team meeting, the manager listens to and appreciates the feedback of their subordinates regarding the evening prior **(introvert)**, and encourages the sharing of opinions while remaining in control of the discussion's direction, when necessary, during conflict or crisis situations **(extrovert)**.

The manager must listen and internalize what all others are saying in order to benefit from their insights **(introvert)**.

Meanwhile, they also assess the underlying dynamics between participants, picking up on subtle details others do not notice **(introvert)** and perceiving what their team needs **(introvert)**.

If this is a good motivational speech, the manager is happy to deliver and uplift team spirits **(extrovert)**.

After this meeting, managers must consider everything they learned and internally process their conclusion **(introvert)**.

They return to their desk to dedicate several hours to focused brainstorming and creating a comprehensive new plan with all that they have learned at the meeting **(introvert)**.

They then must communicate these findings back to the team and delegate tasks focused on working towards greater objectives, ensuring employees understand their project requirements and deadlines **(extrovert)**.

Most of the subordinate- or client-facing roles in the previous description required extroverted tendencies, while the introverted tasks occurred internally and/or alone. Combined with the culture of personality, the public presentation of the extroverted tasks that executives must perform helps to explain why our corporate world has, in the past, favoured the extrovert for leadership roles—this culture creates the impression that these jobs comprise mostly extrovert-friendly requirements due to the visibility of this side of their personalities.

Carolyn Dewar, senior partner at McKinsey & Co., coauthor of a *New York Times* bestseller book on CEO leadership, *CEO Excellence: The Six Mindsets That Distinguish the Best Leaders from the Rest*, and an all-around CEO leadership expert, agrees that there is a misconception about the communication style of leaders:

There is the common wisdom you must be a charismatic, extroverted leader. I think there is actually a real mix! I think that leadership style can be different, not everyone has to be the rah-rah kind of town hall person. It is as much about being self-aware in this context.

Given their unequal starting points and the disadvantages introverts have faced in the past, the process of achieving flexibility and a moderate position on the introvert-extrovert spectrum offers diverse obstacles for each archetype. As we add additional details into consideration (such as the department, the industry, or external workplace trends), the nature of the task and its ideal communication approach might change. For instance, the COVID-19 pandemic further complicated this dynamic and created new implications for extroverts forced to work remotely. More on this in the following chapter.

Clearly, executives can benefit from extroverted or introverted qualities depending on the context. Those who can become more flexible in their identification of and approach to each scenario will almost certainly be more effective.

Tailoring Behaviour to the Needs of Your Team

> It's not about you and what you want to be today. The question is, what do people need you to be today in order to bring out the best in them? Some days the good of the people around you requires extroversion and other days it requires introversion.
>
> Peter Simons (CEO of Simons, a department store chain of over 18 locations and over 3,000 employees, Peter is the third generation of the family to run the chain)

The executive's right-hand people are among their most vital tools.

Paul Sislian (Executive VP of Operations and Operational Excellence at Bombardier Aviation, leading corporate jet maker with over 18,000 employees) believes that the formulation of a strong inner circle is paramount to successful decision-making. His recommendation is the following:

> Do you trust your instinct? Use your judgment and rely on the experts around you. No one man can make every decision. You should surround yourself with the smartest people. I love smart people around me because it challenges me to be smarter, too. Plus, if they have the right answer, why not? That's great."

How does one build the best team? An excellent starting point is: be the best manager. A leader attuned to and willing to support the needs of their subordinates is much more likely to attract and keep a strong group of right-hand people than one who is dismissive of these needs.

In the context of transformational and transactional leadership, Hamstra et al. found that tailoring leadership to followers' preferences may contribute to workforce stability and organizational effectiveness.[10] Similarly, Haumer et al.'s study on message tailoring found that employee engagement is improved when messages fit the needs of different personality types.[11]

Conversely, the opposite effect occurs when messages are incompatible with employee personalities. We argue here that a dynamic communication style is also a prominent vehicle through which a good leader can display their support and earn loyalty from a strong team of subordinates.

Just as there often exists an optimal leadership approach to deal with specific assignments, there also exist favourable communicative strategies for various group dynamics between or with specific members of a team. Some employees prefer a hands-on, extroverted approach, while others are receptive to a less aggressive, introverted style. To be an effective team player and leader, one must identify the different work-style preferences of team members and act accordingly. More in the next chapters on this issue of managing introverts and extroverts differently, both in the context of people who work for you, your peers and managing upward.

Jeff Courey, President and CEO at George Courey Inc., believes that, "It is important for a leader to recognize their staff who are introverts or extroverts—how they receive recognition, praise, and anything else."

Once again, awareness is paramount. Perceiving the preferred communication styles of team members requires diligent observation, understanding when they are more comfortable, and becoming familiar with their work style, which are all essential. When in doubt, asking team members to clarify their preferred environment also works well. Karl has found it helpful with his teams to briefly present the idea of the three types and have each person on the team discuss their preferences so the manager can manage in a more appropriate way, and they can work with one another and know how to better manage upward.

Willie Walsh, the former CEO of British Airways and CEO of IATA, the International Airline Transport Association, headquartered in Geneva, uses a noteworthy strategy to encourage contributions from his quieter employees during group meetings. He believes in the anarchy of opinions, that no one opinion is above another, and all should be heard and considered equally. In his view, everyone on his team offers valuable additions to the discussion, although he does not require verbal participation or evaluate contribution by how much his subordinates speak. However, some cases present an exception.

Walsh explains: "I had one team member who worked for me. He was very bright. I liked his thinking because he tended to be contrarian in his views, but he was an introvert."

For this particular individual, Walsh would look for a nonverbal sign that he had something to contribute, and would then invite him to speak in the discussion. Walsh's situational awareness allowed him to notice such employees, a skill that might seem obvious but is often overlooked amidst the demands of everyday leadership. This particular attention made his employees feel valued, fostering loyalty and creating a more cohesive and effective team.

According to Walsh, "When he spoke, everybody listened to what he had to say." In our experience, this is often the situation when people are known for not speaking too easily or quickly when they do speak, we pay more attention because it is a bit more unusual, and they tend to have quite insightful things to say. Partly because they listened to other people's comments and then often pulled together disparate thoughts into a new insight.

Walsh took extra care to identify the specific needs of one of his employees and acted to ensure these needs were met. The actions taken in this scenario were to the benefit of the whole team: given the brilliance of the employee's perspective on certain challenges discussed, the group could understand their points through the uncommon lens of the introverted employee, thereby ensuring a comprehensive analysis of the issue at hand and a more thorough deliberation of potential solutions.

Introvert and Extrovert Breaks

As we have said a few times, the central idea behind introversion and extroversion is our response to stimulation. Introverts gain energy when by themselves; the opposite is true for extroverts. When an introvert is required to act like an extrovert, or vice versa, the higher level of effort required to operate outside their comfort zone can drain their energy at a rapid pace. To recharge their batteries, an introvert may choose to take a walk by themselves, read a book, put on headphones when they are on a flight or commuting home on the subway, or simply close their office door for some time alone. These practices are known as "introvert breaks," and they are widely recognized as strategies to cope with a business world known to traditionally favour the louder, more social, extroverted personality type.

Frank Kollmar, former president and CEO of L'Oreal Canada and now Deputy General Manager for Global Active Cosmetics Division at L'Oréal, a top global position, posits that a long-term career as a high-level manager requires you to "know where your energy sources are." His preferred form of introverted break is spending time with family or in nature.

On the other hand, when an extrovert must act introverted for an extended period of time, perhaps when working long hours alone at their desk, they might need to seek out opportunities to interact with other people. Group work sessions, meetings, networking socials, or colleague dinners are all great opportunities for extroverts to recharge via social engagement. We refer to these as "extrovert breaks," a relatively new idea, albeit one that has been a part of the lives of extroverts forever.

Introvert and extrovert breaks are essential for executives in two dimensions. We will discuss extrovert breaks again a bit later in Chapters 5–7.

First, an executive's greater awareness of the social style of their subordinates allows them to remain sensitive to employee needs in the daily operations of an organization. One key component of effectively working with others is being conscious of the need for people to take introverted or extroverted breaks, and giving them the opportunities to do so. For a manager of introverts, perhaps it means giving your employees some well-deserved space and respecting their need for isolation. For a manager of extroverts, on the other hand, this strategy could involve chatting with your employee at the water cooler or over a cup of coffee, respecting their need for interaction. We will delve into more specific tips for dealing with those on both sides of the continuum in later sections of this book.

Second, executives must be sure to practice mindfulness regarding their own social battery, taking introverted or extroverted breaks as needed in order to ensure that they can function to the best of their leadership capabilities.

Paul Speed, CEO and co-founder of Kyoto Brewing Company in Japan, is an introvert who has learned to approach certain challenges as an extrovert. Amidst all of this, however, he remains committed to taking the time to recharge and return when ready to be his best: "Depending upon the situation and expectation of the person you are talking to, sometimes you've got to work the room. But at the end of the day, I like just to hole up and read my book."

A greater understanding of the needs of subordinates offers substantial opportunities. Not only can the executive use this information to create an environment which boosts employee morale and work productivity, but they can also use it to reduce inefficiency and increase synergies for collaboration. For instance, here is what Matt Gavin wrote in the Harvard Business School Online:

> I really like having good EQ and understanding how to adjust your approach based on the team. If you have an introverted leader who is a reflective thinker, pairing them with [an employee] who is more extroverted to provide balance can be effective. Sometimes the combination does not work if nobody, or if too many people are willing to step up.[12]

Tailoring Your Behaviour to Environmental and Sociocultural Circumstances

In today's globalized business environment, effective leaders are those who can tailor their behaviour to fit the cultural and social expectations of different contexts. While some individuals naturally thrive in environments that align with their personality—be it introverted or extroverted—leadership often requires adaptability. Leaders must navigate the delicate balance between staying true to their natural inclinations and adjusting to meet the demands of their roles. This is especially true when managing diverse teams or working across regions where cultural norms around communication and social interaction can vary widely.

Narayana Murthy, the founder of the Indian IT giant Infosys, provides a compelling example of this adaptability. Known for his introverted tendencies, Murthy shares how he learned to engage in social interactions to achieve his business goals. For him, schmoozing was a skill he developed out of necessity rather than preference, demonstrating the flexibility required of leaders in competitive industries. Indeed, Narayana Murthy had to step outside his natural comfort zone and embrace behaviours that didn't come easily to him as an introvert:

> To grow the firm, you had to work in the room, you had to schmooze people. You learned to do that and you were good at it, but it would tire you out.

In a business environment that favoured extroverted qualities like networking and public engagement, Narayana Murthy learned to connect with people. This wasn't about changing who he was; it was about meeting the demands of his role:

> I did it because there was a goal. As long as that goal requires me to be articulate; as long as that goal requires me to schmooze with people; as long as that goal does not require me to do anything unethical or illegal, I will do it. But if I have to relax then I don't have to go to somebody. I'm quite happy reading and sitting listening to music on my own.

The scenarios previously described reflect the common challenges faced by leaders across many North American industries. However, it is essential to recognize that additional factors may influence a leader's approach to communication. Regional cultural expectations, specific industry standards, and varying degrees of acceptance for introverted or extroverted behaviour can all shape how a leader chooses to interact with others. In some cultures, assertive networking might be celebrated, while in others, a more reserved approach is preferred. Effective leaders are those who understand these nuances and can adjust their communication style accordingly, ensuring they resonate with their audience while remaining authentic to their own personality.

Similarly, Faisal Kazi, President and CEO of Siemens Canada, has navigated unique challenges in modelling his leadership style to various environmental and sociocultural expectations. His career at Siemens spanned over three decades and included leadership roles in many different countries across the world, including Germany, the Netherlands, China, Brazil, the Philippines, Mexico, and the United States. As he thrived in a highly competitive environment in so many different places, Kazi has developed a real expertise at tailoring his behaviour to align with both his personal strengths and the particular demands of different cultural and professional settings. He gives us his precious insight:

> As a CEO of a multinational company, I've had to balance staying true to my personality with adapting to the cultural demands of various regions. Each time I move to a new country, I make an effort to learn the local culture with as open a mindset as possible. No culture is perfect, I've come to realize— each has elements that feel more natural and others that require adjustment. The most important thing, however, is to maintain an open perspective and avoid falling into judgment. Adjusting to a new culture is about embracing what it has to offer, knowing that there is always something positive to gain from it.
>
> For instance, adapting to North American culture came with its own set of challenges. In my previous roles, especially in Germany, I had learned that discussions should be precise and concise; speaking more than necessary could be perceived as a sign of weakness. But in North American culture,

holding the floor and speaking at length is often seen as a way to demonstrate expertise and confidence. This difference required me to adjust my communication style to align with the expectations of my North American teams and stakeholders. It was an interesting shift that reinforced the importance of cultural adaptability in leadership.

For executives, the key takeaway from this subchapter is the value of sociocultural and behavioural adaptability. Leaders who can balance their own personality traits with the demands of diverse environments are better equipped to connect with their teams, communicate effectively, and build trust across borders. This adaptability is a core competency in the modern business world, and it can help leaders succeed in any sociocultural context.

By Country or Region

Perhaps the most obvious diverse circumstance is culture, which differs by region and country as it is derived from a particular area's specific environmental and geopolitical factors. Hofstede and McCrae (2004) conducted a study at IBM that quantified the differences between cultures as manifested in dominant value systems and the effects of these factors on business operations.[13] Mean personality scores from 33 countries were found to be correlated with culture dimensions' scores. By association, any differences in communication style associated with various personalities also pertain to some level of cultural influence. Their work suggested four key dimensions by which cultures can differ from each other: individualism and collectivism, power distance, uncertainty avoidance and masculinity and femininity. The Globe work, based on research in 62 countries, went beyond Hofstede's pioneering work to add a few more dimensions: these dimensions include power distance, uncertainty avoidance, institutional collectivism, in-group collectivism, gender egalitarianism, assertiveness, future orientation, performance orientation, and humane orientation.

Differences in work-style preferences are dramatic across borders. It is important to keep this in mind while doing business in general, as positive international relationships are more likely to form based on mutual understanding and respect for the cultures of others. This lesson is also useful in the context of this book's focus, as communication style is a common and immediate vehicle for showing and earning respect.

North American society prefers extroversion. Other countries, such as those in Asia, tend to be more introverted in contrast. A consciousness of these cultural differences and the ability to adapt behaviours accordingly are equally imperative in light of increasing globalization in the corporate and political worlds.

Some cultures are more introverted, others more extroverted. Karl knows one introvert joke, which he will now share. His mother was Finnish. How do you tell a Finnish introvert from a Finnish extrovert? A Finnish introvert looks at your shoes when she is talking to you, a Finnish extrovert looks at your shoes when she is talking to you. Karl has also taught in Iceland at Reykjavik University a number of times. When he mentions this joke in class, it seems to resonate with them when it comes to Icelandic culture, a bit more of an introverted culture.

There are also more extroverted societies. Karl recently presented this research at the American University in Cairo to a group of about 25 Egyptian senior executives. Their consensus opinion was that Egypt, at least Cairo, the great urban centre of the country, is more to the extroverted side. Many had worked in other countries, one mentioned working for many years in Belgium, his view, supported by other Belgians we have discussed this with, is that Belgium tends to be a more introverted country. Of course, it is possible that the most extroverted person in the world is Belgian and the most introverted person you know is Egyptian. So, every culture and country's population have the bell curve shape of introverts, ambiverts and extroverts. To some degree, it is about social norms, what is acceptable behaviour in a society.

As an example of the divergent range of communication styles across regional cultures, we would like to compare the recent interviews of two prominent executives.

According to Stephany Fier, VP of Exploration and Technical Services at SilverCrest Metals Inc. in Vancouver, there exists an extreme cultural tendency towards extroversion south of the US border: "I like talking to people, hearing about other people's experiences. I love managing everybody down in Mexico. To be doing business in a Latin American country, you are not allowed to be much of an introvert."

Conversely, we conducted an interview with Shobhita Soor, the introverted CEO and founder of Legendary Foods Africa, while visiting West Africa on our annual Hot Cities of the World Tour. She revealed something completely different about the business culture of Ghana: "Being timid or soft-spoken is not a negative. I would say, within the culture, people would probably still perceive me as an extrovert because it is more common to be soft-spoken."

Although these two women manage in entirely different industries, their individual insights are equally valuable. Latin American and West African cultural diversions in communication style are only one variation of several regions that exhibit cultural and, thus, communication style differences. It is important to be aware of the cultural environment in which one operates their business and how to adjust behaviour in accordance with particular regional traditions and practices.

Canada tends to be more introverted overall, though Calgary may be more extroverted thanks to the influence of Americans and others working in the oil industry.

Figure 3.1 from Vividmaps.com shows the percentage of extroverts in the states of the United States. When shown this map most people are not

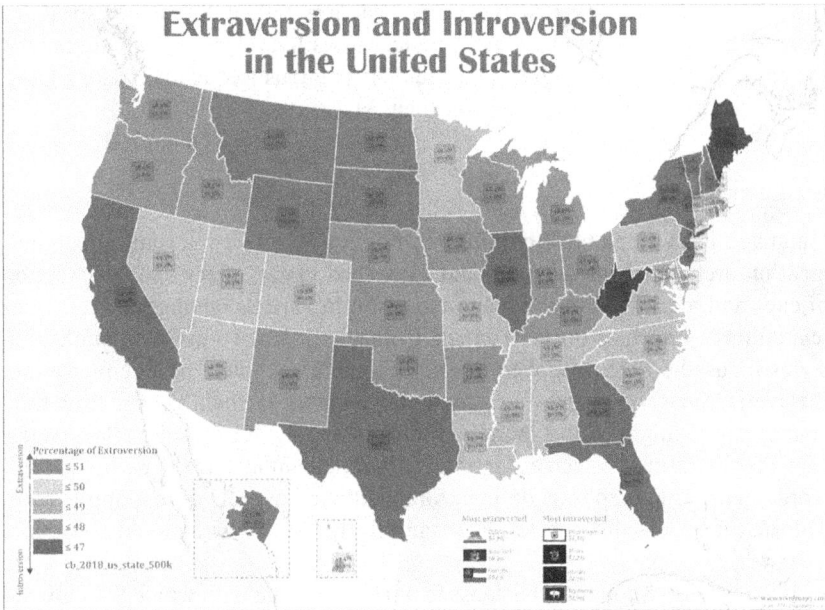

Figure 3.1 Extroversion and Introversion in the United States[14]

surprised that the more extroverted states include New York, Texas, Florida, Illinois, and California. Though in these states, there are also many, many introverts as well.

An executive of a transnational organization must remain sensitive to the cultural differences of employees working at a company's foreign location(s). If executives are appreciative of these differences and learn to work with them, they are more likely to earn praise at the international level within their organization, and also to streamline any opportunities for promotion to a level of multinational management.

A great new book came out in spring 2024 from Portfolio/Penguin by Jessica Chen entitled *Smart, Not Loud: How to Get Noticed at Work for All the Right Reasons*. Jessica is an Emmy Award winner, keynote speaker and CEO of Soulcast, a global business communication training agency. Prior to starting Soulcast, she was a broadcast television journalist. In her excellent book, she compares quiet cultures and loud cultures. She makes the point, which we very much agree with, that one is not better than the other. She writes, "both are equally valued and needed." She makes the point that it goes beyond just being an introvert or extrovert; it is about values and beliefs taught by family and culture during your formative years. In what she calls a quiet culture, people are told from an early age to follow instructions, listen to others, talk less and let their words speak for themselves. She contrasts this to what she calls a loud culture, who are taught, she argues, virtually the opposite: share their opinions frequently, make a lot of noise, and carve out opportunities for themselves.

By Language

Language is an element of culture that might also affect our natural communication archetype. Introversion and extroversion can affect one's perception of cues and meanings during communication in various languages. High context cultures—such as those of Japan, China, and Brazil—use communication styles focused on the unspoken meaning, tone, and context of a conversation. Introverts, possessing greater situational awareness than their extroverted counterparts, might adjust better to understanding high-context languages. Low context cultures, such as German culture, communicate primarily through words, with little emphasis on the aforementioned aspects of communication. This might be less difficult to understand for those with situational awareness weaknesses.

If an executive conducts business in a new language with which they are not comfortable, they usually exhibit slightly less certainty in their choice of words and may act more introverted than normal.

Alex Brzotowski, Director of Consulting Services at CGI, an over 90,000-person IT giant headquartered out of Montréal, has experienced a shift in communication tendencies by switching languages,

> I would say I am extroverted, but I feel this is something that changes at a time. When I was in Montreal, where I was working in a French language area, I felt less confident due to my language skills, so I became more introverted. Since moving back home to the US, I have shifted back towards being an extrovert, but less so than I was before.

In Brzotowski's circumstance, his experience in Montréal left an imprint on his communication style, which lasted even after returning to a place of work where his native tongue dominated. Perhaps Brzotowski established a lasting growth mindset, which shifted his position on the introvert-extrovert continuum to one more moderate than before. Such a transition is likely to have provided an overall benefit for Brzotowski and his work mentality.

When an executive, like Alex Brzotowski, conducts business in a new language with which they are not as comfortable, they usually exhibit slightly less certainty in their choice of words and may act more introverted than normal. Alex, an Australian who has spent years working in Canada and now the US, has evolved his style over time.

By Industry

> It's important to have different personalities, different backgrounds, and different cultures. It's the thing that excites me about the airline industry.
>
> Willie Walsh (Director General of IATA, the International Airline and Aviation Association, ex-CEO of British Airways)

While general recommendations remain the same as we move between industries, it is important to acknowledge a few key potential differences in the industry cultures where businesses operate. On occasion, people of similar personalities and communication styles concentrate within one particular field due to a mutual interest in certain topics of study. This collection of like-minded individuals has the potential to encourage a continuous loop of similar personalities joining a field, eventually forming a stereotype for that particular position. As they cluster within an industry, they begin to affect the dynamics of said industry. This trend is especially relevant to us if these individuals fall within a similar realm of the introvert-extrovert continuum.

Extroverts tend to thrive in businesses where they are rewarded for active engagement with their environment. These circumstances are common in industries such as sales, PR, politics and government, law, and business.

Contrarily, introverts prefer environments where they are rewarded for active internal engagement, primarily in activities that are predominantly evident in industries of a creative nature and require complex problem-solving or specialty skills. These fields are usually niche and require specific expertise because, as explained in the prior chapter, introverts are capable of spending long hours devoted to projects and mastering skills.

This is not to say that an individual entering an environment or industry with other entrants dissimilar to themselves is unlikely to be successful. Rather, this individual has the potential to shine as a unique asset to the company, as long as they become well aware of and prepared to replicate the more common qualities present in the industry in addition to their uncommon traits.

For example, say an extroverted type enters an introvert-dominant creative industry such as data mining or computer engineering. As long as the extrovert becomes familiar with the normal tendencies and practices of this industry, such as internalized thought processing and decision-making, long hours of focused dedication, and time spent alone, they have the opportunity to stand out from others using their natural tendencies, which are relatively uncommon among others in this field. Instinctively, they are more likely than their peers to speak up and lead a meeting, assert their ideas to superiors, or take control of a situation during potential crises. These qualities are unique to the industry and will serve them well. This example exhibits a scenario that perfectly explains why striking a balance is such a beneficial approach to success in the corporation. The same could be said for an introvert in the sales department, who may be seen as uniquely authentic, concise, thoughtful, and aware of the client's needs.

You might be comforted to learn that we observed a similar pattern among the high-level generals we interviewed during our reconnaissance phase. The systemic masculine, power-focused, dominant-adjacent reputation of the military has attracted large populations of loud (and perhaps aggressive at times) extroverts. Such an influx of this persona has encouraged a stereotype of authoritative, hardline generals, as we often see depicted in historical war films or comically caricatured in cartoons. By contrast, all of the generals we have spoken with are self-proclaimed introverts. Again, they exhibit a prime example of the value of striking a balance, especially in cases where it is difficult or unnatural to do so.

In an interview for this book General Giles Hill, a former senior British Army officer, suggests that "[he has] come to the conclusion from different people's observations that [his] quiet, reflective type has tended to help address complicated leadership challenges in a way that outgoing types have been less able to do."

Because their more introverted nature contrasts with the authoritative, noisier, more hardline extrovert cliché that we commonly associate with the role, introverts practiced their nondominant persona and were able to utilize their natural tendencies as a means to set themselves apart from the rest. As learned ambiverts, they serve as a perfect symbol for the argument of this book.

We also spoke to General John Rutherford Allen, retired US Marine Corps four-star general and former commander of NATO. As a natural introvert, he told us that,

> When I am out, engaging and speaking, and sharing my thoughts and bringing the team along—this is an important part of what I do, part of being a leader. But for me, on a Saturday morning to have a coffee and a book, that is a little slice of heaven.

Our Key Takeaways

#1 Flexibility and awareness separate executives and strong managers from other employees.

Our interviews show that most executives have developed two traits that are highly valuable and pertinent to their success: situational awareness and the capacity to balance their introverted and extroverted qualities to achieve flexibility. These managers can sense when their approach to a situation must change, and they are capable of adapting with the appropriate behaviour.

#2 The growth mindset and the free traits theory transform a complex situation into an opportunity to improve.

As CEOs discover new and diverse environments with their growth mindset, they tend to learn and master the practices necessary for good leaders. By implementing the free traits theory, they do not remain stuck in the determined pattern of their personality but act in a manner appropriate to their context and employees' needs. Thus, by becoming increasingly aware and flexible, CEOs are capable of promoting the advancement of a particular goal or strategy for their company's or their own prosperity.

#3 The learning curve associated with familiarity in uncomfortable environments pays off in the long run.

An individual entering an environment or industry largely populated with others dissimilar to themselves has the potential to shine as a more unique asset to the company, as long as they become proficient with the more common important qualities present in the industry.

Notes

1 Raja, Farhan, Akhtar, Dr., and Hussain, Syed. "Exploring Perception of Professionals Regarding Introversion and Extroversion in Relation to Success at Workplace." *Journal of Educational Sciences & Research* 7, no. 2 (Fall 2020): 184–195.
2 Tjan, A. K. "How Leaders Become Self-Aware." *Harvard Business Review*, 2012.
3 Tjan, A. K. (2012).
4 Little, Brian R. "Personal Projects and Free Traits: Personality and Motivation Reconsidered." *Social and Personality Psychology Compass* 2, no. 3 (2008): 1235–1254.
5 Little, Brian R. (2008).
6 Little, Brian R. (2008).
7 Little, Brian R. (2008).
8 Little, Brian R. (2008).
9 Dweck, Carol S. *Mindset: The New Psychology of Success.* New York: Ballantine Books, 2007.
10 Hamstra, Melvyn R. W., et al. "Transformational-Transactional Leadership Styles and Followers' Regulatory Focus." *Journal of Personnel Psychology* 10, no. 4 (2011): 182–186.
11 Haumer, Florian, et al. "Tailor the Message and Change Will Happen? An Experimental Study of Message Tailoring as an Effective Communication Strategy for Organizational Change." *Journal of Strategy and Management* 14, no. 4 (2021): 426–443.
12 Gavin, Matt. "Authentic Leadership: What It Is & Why It's Important." *Harvard Business School Online Business Insights Blog*, December 10, 2019.
13 Hofstede, Geert and McCrae, Robert R. "Personality and Culture Revisited: Linking Traits and Dimensions of Culture." *Cross-Cultural Research* 38, no. 1 (2004): 52–88.
14 Egoshin, Alex. Permission granted for data from *Vivid Maps* (June 2022). Accessed November 10, 2024.

Chapter 4

Striking a Balance in Today's World

I sit on the line, Karl. I get a lot of energy from being out with people. Having the house open on a weekend and people coming and going is a joy. But equally, with my job and my work, I need time to stop and reflect and just think. And cycling sometimes gives me that. If I do go out on my own, just time to step back and slow down a little bit. So I think I sit on the line and I move between the two.

Ivan Vella (CEO, Rio Tinto, a global mining firm
with over 57,000 employees)

Recent trends have led us to re-evaluate the ideal communication style in today's corporate workforce. Susan Cain's emphasis on introverts and their unique traits still holds significant merit and remains a valuable critique of our systemic inclination towards extroverted leaders. However, in the 13 years since *Quiet*'s publication, we believe that various influences in Western society today have shifted our collective view of personality to a new place. Giving this trend even more momentum, the COVID pandemic caused significant changes in the corporate world.

We believe that there is considerable value to be obtained from striking a balance in a leader's approach to communication. Thanks to their temperament, ambiverts are naturally inclined to achieve this balance regularly.[1] In our hundreds of interviews with executives, we found that on the bell curve of introversion/extroversion, about 40% were introverted, 40% and 20% were ambiverts. Our initial thought when we heard about ambiverts was that, with three categories, it would be 33%, 33%, and 33%, this was mistaken.

We will discuss ambiverts more fully in the next chapter. They are who we predict to be the most successful in this new generation of the corporation. Or the people, introverted and extroverted, who learn to act like them on a more regular basis.

We would like to consider the impact of COVID on how we work and how this allowed an introvert's approach to be one more broadly accepted and indeed to some degree emulated.

DOI: 10.4324/9781003612216-5

Remote and Hybrid Work: A New Paradigm

The adoption of remote and hybrid work models, accelerated by the COVID-19 pandemic, represents a significant shift for many of us in workplace culture. These models provide employees with the flexibility to choose where and how they work, supporting diverse productivity needs and personal preferences.

Open Space and Its Decline

In a 2019 *Harvard Business Review* article, HBS's Bernstein and MIT's Waber opined,

> The open office layout has become a standard in many workplaces, particularly in tech and creative industries, where collaboration is essential. The design typically features few walls, with senior executives often working alongside their teams in a shared space. The early 2000s marked a significant departure from the cubicle-based office layouts that dominated previous decades, as companies began adopting open office designs to promote collaboration and communication among employees.[2]

However, the actual effects of open-plan offices are often counterproductive, as Susan Cain points out:

> Open-plan offices have been found to reduce productivity and impair memory. They're associated with high staff turnover. Another study of 38,000 knowledge workers across different sectors found that the simple act of being interrupted is one of the biggest barriers to productivity.[3]

Supporting this, Bernstein and Waber in their *Harvard Business Review* found that when companies transitioned to open offices, face-to-face interactions decreased by 70%, while digital communication increased significantly.

Reality Check: The Impact of COVID-19 and Remote Work

While the decline of open spaces began before the COVID-19 pandemic, the global health crisis dramatically accelerated the shift to new kinds of workspaces, especially remote and hybrid work models. Remote work became mandatory for many companies, forcing them to rethink their strategies for maintaining productivity and collaboration. Open spaces no longer held the same value in this new environment, as employees were now working from home.

A Norwegian study highlighted the significant shift in work dynamics during this period. It noted that "employees were forced to work from home (WFH) because office spaces were no longer accessible" and that maintaining social contact and productivity became heavily reliant on digital platforms like Zoom, Skype, and Microsoft Teams.[4] The study further pointed out that a "sense of professional isolation is negatively related to individual job performance," emphasizing the challenges both introverts and extroverts faced in adapting to this new work environment. The lack of physical proximity heightened the need for personal strategies to cope with the sense of disconnection.

We can speculate that this shift may have been easier for introverts, who often prefer solitude and a quieter work environment. Extroverts, on the other hand, had to work very hard at times to maintain productivity and a sense of connection, leveraging virtual interactions to substitute for in-person social engagement. According to the Norwegian study by Danilova et al., the "quality of the home office setup" was crucial to maintaining productivity, with adequate facilities like furniture and equipment playing a significant role in individual performance.

Karl wrote a piece for his *Forbes* blog with a former student of his, Kat Garcia, also very much an extrovert, entitled "'I Can't Take It Anymore!'": How To Cope With The Lockdown As An Extrovert." This was only in March 22, 2020.

We wrote this in response to the first week of social isolation as extroverts. And it was only week one. Working at home during lockdown for Kat Garcia in New York City, and I myself with my family in Montréal, was no easy feat for very extroverted people. So, we came up with five practical suggestions for our fellow extroverts as they battle to tolerate the "restless extrovert" within. Now we have to add the caveat: Kat and I are pretty extreme extroverts.

Introversion/ambiversion/extroversion is a bell curve, and we lie on the far end of the extrovert side of that curve. Most people are closer to the middle, just a bit introverted or extroverted. My research interviews with over 350 C-suite executives suggest that these traits evolved over our lives and that leaders need to be able to act like both at times. But onto our points.

These strategies proved valuable for us during the lockdown, and they remain just as relevant today. As remote work has become more common, these approaches can help extroverts maintain their energy and connection in any kind of work from home or hybrid setting. Here are the five key tips:

Keep your Cadence

Maintaining a daily routine is essential. This might mean setting your alarm clock early to work out in the morning, sitting down to your morning coffee (and maybe video-calling a friend from work), or putting on your office wear (or something other than your pyjamas). Get as fully ready as you normally would to prepare yourself mentally for the workday. Pretend you are going into the office. Make your workspace one you want to work in—have a great setup that makes you want to get to work. Some firms are providing some funding to help do this; ask your organization. Arrange all of the things you would have at hand in your usual office space: pen and paper, your computer and phone, some water and a hot beverage, and whatever else you need. For video calls, consider putting up a picture behind you that represents your city, instead of showing a messy home background.

Tap Into Your Entrepreneurial Spirit

Working remotely or from home allows downtime and reflection, which can boost creativity. You can finally work through your to-do list in peace or even go as far as creating a new business venture! Kat, who founded *The Corporate Diary*, a blog where she interviews women in business while sharing her own personal journey as she navigates the corporate world, has kept busy creating new content alongside an additional project. She and her friend, Dahye Jung, a strategy analyst at Sidlee, established "Ladies Who Lunch (from home)," a virtual community for women who work in the corporate world to meet and chat about topics unrelated to the virus to spread positivity and connection. In both of our experiences, and to our surprise, a virtual lunch can be almost as fulfilling and fun as an actual lunch and much less expensive!

Create a Solid Social Calendar

Schedule virtual meetups to maintain a sense of social connection. Many people are still participating in virtual breakfasts, "quarantinis," online game nights, live virtual yoga sessions, or other fitness classes with instructors via social media, and more. You can also reach out to elderly family members, neighbours, and acquaintances who might feel isolated. Social isolation has serious negative health implications that are particularly hard on seniors. Give them a ring to lift their spirits and your own!

Build a Sense of Community Outdoors

Generate a real sense of community when you do step outside. While Zoom, Google Hangouts, WebEx, FaceTime, and all virtual video conferencing platforms are great tools to utilize at a time like this, it's no secret that extroverts need a physical sense of community, too. Making time in the day to take ten to 15-minute walks outside of your home is crucial—especially if you live alone. In my case, after almost 20 years in the same neighbourhood, just chatting with neighbours who happen to be in the street at the same time is great. These conversations can recharge your extrovert batteries and create a better sense of belonging, which is often lacking in a city.

Unwind as You Would Normally

Extroverts still need to rest from social interactions as others do. Unwinding from Zoom calls, screen time, and constant exposure to technology by taking some time away is essential. Meditating, journaling, taking a bath, or cooking alone are all ways to distance oneself from the constant noise. This is especially true for a family person like me, as constantly sharing a house with others can be overwhelming. The noise of four adults in a house can be too much, even for an extrovert. Extroverts, like introverts, need quiet time to think, and in my case, finish off a book (this book is coming five years later—so it didn't help as much as Karl thought!). Kat suggested the bath idea; I'm still not so sure about that one, but it works for her!

These tips were originally developed during a period of intense social isolation, but they continue to hold value today. As remote work becomes a more permanent fixture in our lives, these strategies offer practical ways for extroverts to maintain their social energy and productivity outside of a traditional office setting. For many, the sense of disconnection experienced during the lockdown mirrors the isolation that can occur in any remote work environment, making these approaches broadly applicable to modern, flexible work arrangements.

Hybrid Work: A New Model for Post-Pandemic Productivity

As workplaces reopen, many employees are choosing to continue working from home by preference rather than necessity. According to research reported in the *Econopol Policy Brief*, 56% of employees now prefer hybrid work arrangements, where they split their time between home and the office, while 26% wish to work from home full-time.[5] Hybrid work offers a balance between collaboration and solitude, making it an ideal model for accommodating both introverts and extroverts.

For introverts, hybrid work provides the opportunity to engage in focused, independent work at home without the social pressures of the office. Extroverts, conversely, can use their in-office days to satisfy their need for social interaction. Bernstein and Weber's *Harvard Business Review* study on the drawbacks of both remote work and open offices points out that remote work "tends to inhibit collaboration even over digital channels," which can particularly challenge extroverts.[6] Thus, hybrid work strikes a balance, offering structured opportunities for face-to-face interactions while allowing the flexibility to work in solitude when necessary.

The global study by Askoy and colleagues on WFH practices found that 62% of respondents cited socializing as the top benefit of working at business premises, while 60% considered the absence of a commute the most significant advantage of WFH.[7] This further supports the idea that hybrid work accommodates both personality types, enabling employees to enjoy the best of both worlds.

The Relevance of Ambiversion

What does this shift to hybrid work mean for leadership in today's world? Executives and managers must recognize that neither introverts nor extroverts have an inherent advantage in these new environments.

The Fall of the Extrovert: Culture of Personality

Our society's industrial roots, as cited by Cain, remain. However, we have partially transitioned to a knowledge-based economy in which growth is dependent on the quality of available information rather than the means of production.[8] The knowledge economy is a system dependent on the intellectual capabilities of its participants rather than physical inputs or natural resources. In this new system, Big Data analytics and automation, instead of traditional inputs, are fundamental to the production process.

Susan Cain dubbed the culture of personality as the era caused by the increased anonymity of relationships during America's urbanization. She correctly labels this shift in society as a foundation for the predominant preference for extroverted leaders (as we discussed in Chapter 1). Anonymity still exists today, albeit in a much different form. Instead of minimal information on citizens in society, there now exists limitless vaults of data on each individual. In addition to our physical world, we now live in a virtual realm with unlimited access to information. We are anonymous in the sense that we have become single quantitative data points in a vault with millions of others just like us. Our relationships with specific individuals, however, are no longer as anonymous as before.

One may learn about the reputation of potential friends and opponents online before ever meeting them. The performance data, quarterly reports, and previously hidden (or at least, difficult to access) details of a company are now all available to the average person after a short session of internet browsing. Social media platforms like LinkedIn and Facebook allow users to establish connections on extended networks for business and personal use. Sometimes, such connections are purely virtual and are not borne by interactions with others in real life. We are very familiar with this phenomenon, as we have sourced the individuals interviewed for this book largely using Karl's online networks, like LinkedIn.

What is the implication of this change? Industrial America's problem of anonymity no longer exists in the same way. The confident "go-getter" persona of the culture of personality's coveted extrovert is the solution to a problem on the decline. Although extroverted traits were previously a necessity to promote oneself and establish relationships with strangers, society seems to have grown beyond their preference for the extrovert—although this is not to say that this personality type is not still advantageous in some situations.

Susan Cain's work remains invaluable to the study of communication and leadership. The culture of personality lives on, and its preference for extroversion is systemic. Because our systems are built around it, we will experience its effects for years to come. For example, the manner in which many individuals and corporations advertise themselves online is a remnant of the culture of personality's boastful nature. Our affinity for Hollywood culture and our unwavering interest in celebrities are also illustrations of the culture's integration into our daily lives. Thus, the culture of personality is still very much an important factor to consider in our analysis.

Nevertheless, a new issue has emerged in our society: unlimited data and information are instantly available for our purview—although much of this information is unfortunately inaccurate or misleading. We face a problem of inauthenticity. The deceitful advertisements of companies striving for higher sales volumes, the rise of fake news and waning trust in politicians, and a growing emphasis on conspiracies against climate change that demonstrate the truth as relative rather than factual are all manifestations of our new challenge. Drowned in a never-ending cycle of contradictory information, we no longer know what is real and what is to be believed.

The extrovert archetype is particularly ill-equipped to tackle this new problem. The qualities we once celebrated in extroverted leadership, namely their capacity to assure and to perform, are not as capable of deciphering fact from fabrication.

If anything, this archetype has only contributed to the problem. We used to trust loud leaders to be in charge, but the reasons for this decision do not hold up in present conditions. There now exists room at the top for other approaches to have a strong voice.

The Introvert's Diminished Competitive Advantage in a Post-COVID World

In previous sections of this book, we have stated that, as a consequence of systemic disadvantages, introverts have been more regularly forced to operate using unnatural qualities in extrovert-friendly environments. As a result, they became well-versed in this practice and attracted the attention of psychologists and strategists alike on account of their unique tendencies and subsequent phenomenal leadership capacities. Their resilience in an extroverted system made them particularly special and successful leadership figures.

Susan Cain led the movement towards a greater appreciation of quiet leaders and the extraordinary management qualities introverts can bring to the conference table. Although this research remains true, COVID-19 altered the corporate environment. Post-pandemic, we require a further reinterpretation of Cain's research.

The value of introverts cannot be entirely credited to the essence of the qualities they possess that extroverted leaders do not; in truth, much of the introvert's recent significance stems from a practiced capability to keep up with their extroverted counterparts in some aspects and to outshine them in others where unique introverted qualities are revealed (and where extroverts, unprepared in these aspects, cannot keep up).

Similar to the scenario of military generals described in the previous chapter, introverted qualities were diamonds in the rough—suddenly excessively valuable in predominantly extroverted environments. Because they practiced and prepared their extroverted skills to live in a society built for loud leaders, their introverted tendencies could uniquely illuminate issues, often in ways that extroverts were incapable of replicating. However, this setting no longer exists so prominently.

The social isolation of the pandemic created a highly difficult environment for extroverts to operate normally. Although the pandemic presented challenges on both sides of the spectrum, it is clear that extroverts fell into a situation that persistently taxed their natural communication preferences like never before. Just ask Karl how difficult his experiences were.

Extroverts gained experience with their introverted sides by spending excess time alone, refraining from social environments, and attempting internal reflection as a coping mechanism for their new reality in a drastically different world. For the first time, extroverts discovered an environment where introverted traits and internal practices had to be explicitly practiced (as introverts so often experienced with extroverted traits pre-2020). Extroverts were presented with an opportunity to catch up with introverts in the practice of nondominant traits, and the competitive advantage for introverted leaders subsequently diminished against those extroverts who took advantage of this chance.

A More Level Playing Field Between Introverts and Extroverts

In our transition to a "new normal" post-pandemic, it has become clear that the world has somewhat transformed. We simply have changed, and we will not be able to return entirely to what was before. Although much of the system built for extroverts remains intact, the problem of authenticity has exposed to us the fact that the extrovert can no longer serve as the "solution" to the culture of personality. As a result, we have become more aware of the faults of this archetype and the times when introverted practices are more appropriate.

Additionally, the pandemic to a considerable degree demanded extroverts to explicitly practice introspection, internal reflection, and other introverted traits. Now, both types have experienced situations in which they were forced to operate in their nondominant region of the continuum.

For convenience purposes or greater sensitivity to less extroverted employees, many of the introvert-friendly systems implemented during the pandemic will remain in place. Remote work has become more prevalent in almost all industries, and the mental health of employees remains an important topic in organizations in a way that was not before the pandemic. About ten years ago, he started asking the CEOs how they kept in shape. Everyone, Karl can't think of an exception, would talk with enthusiasm about how they kept in shape, going to their home gym at 5:30 a.m., riding their bike, swimming, etc. Nowadays, it is much more about overall wellness (both mental and physical) than merely keeping a good physique. In his more recent approach to the question, during the pandemic and even more in the last year or two, Karl has been asking CEOs about how they encourage good mental health habits among their employees, but he also asks them about what they personally are doing about their own mental health. Virtually all answer with considerable enthusiasm and engagement about what they personally are doing. Valerie Pisano, CEO of Mila (Mila: Québec Artificial Intelligence Institute, is recognized worldwide for its major contributions to AI) told Karl how she has practiced meditation several times a week since the pandemic. Meditation, we would like to add, is a highly effective introspective practice, and thus a method for practicing introversion.

However, historical preferences for extroversion are systemic, built into institutions for recruitment, promotion, and work culture. They still exist, even if they are dwindling (to a considerable degree because extroverts are not prepared to solve the new problem of inauthenticity).

What does this all mean? The opportunity for introverts and extroverts to gain a competitive advantage over one another has been reduced because both archetypes have now had some level of experience in environments unfamiliar and uncomfortable to their natural states. Instead, the opportunity for advantage now lies in flexibility—how quickly and seamlessly leaders can alter their communication style on command and as needed. This opportunity for advantage lies with the ambivert.

Ambiverts, being well-practiced in flexibility, are less likely to develop these mechanisms. Medical doctor Domina Petric argues that the ambivert is more likely to tackle challenges with mature defence mechanisms, including humour, anticipation, and altruism.[9] These healthier mechanisms are associated with realistic life goals instead of surrogate goals linked to neurotic mechanisms and based on unrealistic competencies. Ambiverts are flexible, realistic, and aware of themselves, their surroundings, and what they need to do in order to get where they want to go.

Preface to Ambiversion: Ambiversion and Technology

The global shift towards remote work and the increasing reliance on digital communication platforms such as Zoom or Teams have altered the landscape of corporate leadership. The rise of remote work has fundamentally changed the dynamics of team interaction, collaboration, and management. Leaders are now faced with the new challenges and opportunities presented by remote work environments, emphasizing the need for a balanced leadership approach. In this context, ambiverts emerge as ideal examples.

Many firms are implementing a hybrid structure as they emerge from the pandemic: both in-person and remote work are incorporated into the average work week. Remote work necessitates a balance between the impersonal nature of digital communication and the need for personal connection and empathy. These traits, traditionally associated with introverts, become crucial in maintaining team cohesion and understanding individual team members' needs. At the same time, leaders must maintain the charisma and assertiveness associated with extroverts to keep teams motivated and focused, especially in a remote setting where physical presence is absent.

Moreover, technological advancements have transformed traditional leadership roles and the skill sets required to lead effectively in a digital age. Leaders must now quickly adapt to new technologies, lead virtual teams, and maintain employee engagement remotely. This shift calls for a leader who is not just technically proficient but is further capable of managing and motivating teams spread across different locations.

Ambiverts, with their ability to adapt and thrive in both solitary and social settings, are uniquely positioned to meet these contemporary challenges. They can harness their introverted traits to listen actively, show empathy, and give thoughtful responses, while also utilizing their extroverted traits to communicate decisively, engage team members, and drive results. We will dive into the characteristics of ambiverts in the next chapter.

Maslow's Hammer

Before we get into what is the central idea of this book, being like an ambivert, let's first provide a caveat. There is a famous saying, "If the only tool you have is a hammer, you tend to see every problem as a nail."[10] This is a famous quote by Abraham Maslow, which explains a concept commonly known as Maslow's Hammer. It refers to an over-reliance on a familiar or favourite tool. People are wonderfully complex. There are many ways we can look at a colleague, a manager, or an employee as a unique individual. We may consider gender, generation,[11] nationality, profession, time in our organization, title, etc. And it is more subtle than a generation ago, we are apt to recognize more genders and generations than even twenty years ago.

A few years ago, Karl was fixing his back fence. He ran out of nails and lacked a screwdriver (it was down in the basement too far to walk to go get it) and so was hammering in screws to secure the fence boards in place. An elderly neighbour came by and said, "Karl that is wrong!" His point was that a screw is a better fastening device than a nail but it must be screwed in, not hammered in as Karl was doing. Perhaps he was a bit overwrought, but his point was a good one. To be a good handyperson, you need a box of tools, not just a hammer.

In the same way, extroversion/ambiversion/introversion is just one element of a person's personality. There is an abundance of other traits in a personality which either improve or reduce leadership capabilities and mitigate or aggravate potential issues. Ambiverted qualities are merely the hammer in your toolbox, not necessarily the be-all end-all tool solution. So, we need not get carried away.

Now that we have said that, we do recognize that this is seen by many as the most important of the Big Five, and we will proceed to spend the rest of our book on it.

Notes

1 Georgiev, S. Y., Christov, C. V., and Philipova, D. T. "Ambiversion as an Independent Personality Characteristic." *Psychology Journal* 56, no. 3 (2014): 8.
2 Bernstein, Ethan and Waber, Ben. "The Truth About Open Offices: There are Reasons Why They Don't Produce the Desired Interactions." *Harvard Business Review*, November–December 2019.
3 Cain, Susan. *Quiet: The Power of Introverts in a World That Can't Stop Talking.* New York: Crown Publishing Group, 2012, p. 74.
4 Danilova, Kjersti, et al. "Explaining Individual Job Performance in Work From Home (WFH) Arrangements." *Information Technology and People*, July 2022. ResearchGate. https://doi.org/10.1108/ITP-01-2021-0039.
5 Aksoy, C. G., et al. "Working from Home Around the Globe: 2023 Report." *EconPol Policy Brief CESifo* 53 (2023).
6 Bernstein, Ethan and Waber, Ben. (2019).
7 Aksoy, C. G., et al. (2023).
8 Desyatnikov, Ruslan. "Council Post: Management in Crisis: The Best Leadership Style to Adopt in Times of Crisis." *Forbes*, July 17, 2020. www.forbes.com/sites/forbestechcouncil/2020/07/17/management-in-crisis-the-best-leadership-style-to-adopt-in-times-of-crisis/?sh=74f3eccf7cb4.
9 Petric, Domina. "The Introvert-Ambivert-Extrovert Spectrum." *Open Journal of Medical Psychology* 11, no. 3 (2022): 103–111.
10 Maslow, Abraham Harold. *The Psychology of Science: A Reconnaissance.* New York: Harper & Row, 1966. ISBN 978-0-8092-6130-7.
11 Moore, Karl. *Generation Why: How Boomers Can Lead and Learn from Millennials and Gen Z.* Montreal: McGill-Queen's University Press, 2023. In it he argued that people over 45 with a degree were taught a modern worldview and people under 35 with a degree a postmodern worldview and therefore must be managed differently.

Chapter 5

Ambiversion

A Natural Predisposition Towards Balance

Origins of the Ambivert

You know Karl, I think I love people. I'm a little bit of an Ambivert. When I'm out, I'm out. I'm having a lot of fun. I do like to talk to people. I do like to go first and I'm curious about myself. I spend a lot of time by myself when I'm not, you know, in that environment. I run. I don't like to run with anybody else, that's my time. I meditate. I guess I'm very extreme.

David Hopkinson (President, Team Business Operations
at Madison Square Garden Sports Corp. which owns
and operates the NBA Nets team and the NHL Rangers team)

In today's demanding workplace, striking a balance is not all that uncommon. The reality is that although almost everyone sways one way, people fall along the continuum between the extreme introvert and extrovert designations. Jung, father of the terms, states that "There is no such thing as a pure extrovert or introvert—such a man would be in the lunatic asylum."[1]

The ambivert represents a midpoint along the introvert-extrovert continuum. We argue that everyone is amenable to striking some form of balance between their instinctive personality types and the opposite side. In broad terms, therefore, once repositioned centrally to some degree on the spectrum, most people will likely classify themselves as mild versions of the ambivert. We are all ambiverts now, or at least we should be.

Whereas introverts maintain a stronger inward life energy, and extroverts maintain the same thing outwards, ambiverts are characterized by their balance and adaptiveness.[2] The ambivert moves easily between working in groups and working alone, and has a more moderate threshold for sensory stimulation in comparison to their more extreme introvert and extrovert counterparts, who are defined by high and low stimulation, respectively.[3] Therefore, the ambivert easily adjusts their energy to the social context. Petric argues that "ambiversion might be the most adaptive and most stable personality trait in the introversion-extroversion spectrum."[4]

DOI: 10.4324/9781003612216-6

First cited in academic literature in 1924 by psychologist Edward Conklin, the ambivert exhibits "this ability to oscillate between what is clearly introversion and what is clearly extroversion, to find values of life frequently in each phase."[5]

Unfortunately, Conklin's concept failed to gain immediate traction in the academic community. Psychology experts deemed the ambiguity of introverted and extroverted traits in one personality to be less clear-cut for the purpose of scientific research, and too common to produce findings of a nonobvious nature.

York University Professor Ian Davidson labels the ambivert as a personality *non grata* in academia.[6] Davidson explains that the ambivert as a topic of interest survived mostly due to its participation in Eysenck's integrative view of types and traits until it gradually resurfaced as a focus under a new faculty: management leadership.

Adam Grant looked at the ambivert through his lens of sales management in 2013. In his study, Grant aimed to contest the mainstream perspective that extroverted personalities were the best salespeople after he encountered experimental data that was inconclusive with this claim. His findings suggested that ambiverts achieve the strongest sales performance because "they naturally engage in a flexible pattern of talking and listening."[7]

The ambivert exhibits sufficient enthusiasm and assertiveness for persuasion on product purchases, but because they listen to customers' interests and present a trustworthy appearance (not too overconfident or excited in the product offering), they combine the strengths of the introvert and extrovert to increase sales productivity.

After surveying 340 call centre representatives, Grant's study produced an inverted U-shape relationship between extroversion and sales revenue. This demonstrates that, on average, ambivert salespeople tend to perform better than salespeople who are more introverted or extroverted, precisely because ambiverts are more balanced.

In another study focused on sales associates at a sports organization, Furnham and Fudge found similar results.[8] Ambiverts successfully draw on the strengths and advantages of both introverts and extroverts without suffering the debilitating qualities experienced by both extremes.

Henry Mintzberg's Emergent Strategy Versus Michael Porter's Deliberate Strategy—an Ambivert Approach?

What makes the ambivert's qualities so extraordinary? One view that we find particularly compelling is the idea that ambiverts, and introverts to some degree as well, are better at helping deliver the considerable benefits of emergent versus deliberate strategy. In today's turbulent more uncertain world, we believe that an emergent strategy approach wins, in many cases, over a more deliberate strategy. Emergent strategy is championed by Henry Mintzberg, a renowned professor in business strategy at the Desautels Faculty of Management of McGill University, and Karl's colleague and mentor.[9] These notions are not novel, Karl was taught them to some degree during his MBA at USC decades ago, and they remain part of contemporary business curricula. In fact, Karl covers Porter's Three Generic Strategies and his Five Forces Model in his undergraduate strategy course at McGill.

The deliberate strategy approach has been favoured by Harvard's Michael Porter, a longtime rival of Henry's. As you may know, Porter's approach is more CEO centric, with strategy coming from the top. It uses analytic techniques and models like Porter's Five Forces Model,[10] the Three Generic Strategies,[11] the BCG dog, cow, star, and question marks model, Geoffrey Moore's Crossing the Chasm model,[12] etc. Strategy consultants like McKinsey, Bain, and BCG are often used to help the CEO and C-suite executives develop more deliberate strategies. This type of strategic thinking depends on seeing above ("the big picture") and *ahead*. And you need to *think* about strategy to create good strategies, it is about thought and analysis above all. Strategies have to be *formulated* carefully (analytically) and articulated explicitly so that they can then be *implemented* systematically. Indeed, the real problem is in the implementation. So, if it goes wrong the C-suite tends to deflect the blame away from the strategists (themselves) and onto the rest of us, the schmucks, who were tasked with implementing their great strategies—which all too often don't work out. This failure is not just due to poor execution; perhaps, instead, it is because the strategies were not designed for today's world. As a result of our ever-changing world and the rapid pace of revolution and new trends (such as WFH, AI, globalization, etc.), this issue occurs even more frequently now than it did 20 or even 10 years ago.

The world of deliberate strategy is one that Karl remembers well from his days as a corporate manager at IBM and then as an executive teacher at Oxford and LBS. It was a world of strategy planning weekends at posh hotels in the English countryside, where they sat in rooms discussing the Five Forces in their particular industry and what would they change in the model if they had a fairy's magic wand (that is literally one of their key questions, what would they do if they had a magic wand?). The output was three-ring binders in North America and two-ring binders in Europe. This worked well in its day, back in the 80s and part of the 90s, wonderful times now looking back on it, when the past was quite helpful in predicting the future. However, the nature of the world today no longer lends itself, by and large, to this type of strategy.

Emergent strategy is an alternative method to the more traditional approach of deliberate strategy. It is the view that strategy emerges over time as intentions collide with and accommodate a changing reality. Emergent strategy is a set of actions, or behaviour, consistent over time, it is a realized pattern that was not expressly intended in the original planning of strategy. Emergent strategy implies that an organization is learning what works in practice. Given today's world, we believe that emergent strategy is on the upswing. Here's why.

It feels like the relatively stable world of (at least part of) Karl's corporate career has gone the way of the dodo. At times, it seems the world's gone nuts. As one writer put it in the *Sunday New York Times* a few years ago, "For a moment, all the swans seemed black." However, Karl's friend, Dick Evans, CEO of aluminium giant Alcan, who co-taught with Karl the CEO Insights course at McGill for their MBAs for two years, pointed out that Karl's memory was a bit selective, as it was not only recently that stability seems to have gone out the window. He reminded Karl of

> the time Dick was stationed in Africa and experienced three coups—and then back in the USA in the midst of the junk bond raiders, a wrenching manufacturing recession, and the fall of the Iron Curtain—not to mention personally experiencing the Loma Prieta earthquake. All of these seemed pretty 'black swanish' to me at the time!

Fair point; nevertheless, it seems that strategy has shifted in the last decade to where the planning school no longer has the street cred it once had. We cannot, try as we may, control the variables that factor into business decisions. This factor is precisely why Mintzberg's emergent strategy is so useful.

Porter's ideas are still relevant. My colleagues and I still teach them, so I still believe in them, and when I talk to corporate CEOs they still use them as part of their strategy planning thinking. But they are getting a bit long in the tooth for today's different world. Henry's emergent strategy ideas simply seem to be more relevant to the world we live in today—they reflect the fact that our plans will fail. This is not to say that planning isn't useful, but other than some long-term technology plans, the era of the five-year and even two-year plans has faded, and emergent strategy is the reality in most industries that I work with. You must have a much more fleet of feet, strategic flexibility is what we are looking for in most industries. The boundaries are more fluid now. For many, albeit not all, knowing what industry you are in is not as clear-cut as it once was. This also makes industry analysis less easy. The value chain is now shared across firm boundaries and, at times, in part, in common with competitors.

The emergent approach involves a reduced emphasis on formal planning and a greater focus on learning and deliberate adaptation from some of the ideas that are contributed by those from anywhere in the business. This is very much unlike deliberate strategy, which almost entirely comes from the top. In the deliberate approach, anyone in the organization can be a strategist and contribute to the strategy. In an emergent approach, employees at the frontlines of a business are quite important because they have one foot in the organization and one foot firmly in the real world of the customers, suppliers, and competitors. Thus, they are apt to hear about rumours of new entrants and substitutes (you may well recognize that these are the five forces of Porter's Five Forces Model).[13]

A real danger for those at the top of an organization is that they can be insulated from reality by internal meetings, internal reporting, etc. Of course, excellent CEOs try to regularly get out of their corner offices, but the emergent approach puts an even more considerable focus on the front lines—although it is not just the front lines. Anyone in the organization can contribute to the strategy.

Another particularly good source of knowledge comes from issues faced by customers who approach the organization with their problems. These customer issues are often best addressed by cross-functional teams: marketing, manufacturing, customer service, repair people, etc., gather around a conference table and together figure out a real-world solution to the customer's or supplier's issue. This often results in a more creative solution than if only one function addresses an issue by itself. It does call for a bit of humility and listening (hint: ambivert/introvert type skills). This idea is not unlike the one that diversity of skills, communication-based and otherwise, contributes to diversity of discussion and often produces a more developed result.

With emergent strategy, senior managers' job is not to generate ideas, but to be able to spot good ones as they arise from real-world issues (this is often a considerable relief to senior managers when we tell them this!). Their role is then to determine which ones they should resource and disseminate throughout the organization. Senior management has the networks and roles/power to enable them to spread ideas, one instance where hierarchy can be put to particularly good use.

When it works, which is usually the case, the result is a more resilient strategy that is capable of surviving and adapting to the tumultuous circumstances of the business world as it is experienced by frontline employees. COVID-19 provided the perfect setting to cement the legitimacy of emergent strategy as an approach to strategic management.

Mintzberg's view of strategy fits with this book on the topic of ambiversion. The success of the ambivert is sourced from their flexibility in response to various environmental circumstances. This greater awareness of their surroundings acts as the ambivert's frontline receptors, detecting the need for change in their approaches to decision-making, teamwork, or problem-solving. Their toolkit of both introverted and extroverted qualities allows for greater adaptability to the situation at hand, thus resulting in a stronger capacity to reap the benefits of deliberately *striking the balance* on the introverted-extroverted spectrum.

Natural Versus Learned Ambivert

I'm clearly an ambivert, all the cycle tests that I have done put me in the center. I get really reenergized in meetings, especially when we are talking about the growth of the organization, and about how we can do better in the new processes. I also need my personal moments—time for me to write, to reflect, to prepare. And so if I don't do it I won't have time for myself during the day, and I will have insomnia. I need not because I'm stressed but because I just need to reflect.

Marie-Josée Desrocher (CEO of Place des Arts, Canada's
leading centre for the performing arts)

We suspect that the field of psychology neglected the study of ambiverts for a reason. We have been able to explain common traits of introverts and extroverts as backed by neuroscience and experimental evidence. Ambiverts, who occupy a central position on the introvert-extrovert continuum, however, are difficult to identify and explain. They are merely a group in the middle of two extremes.

The ideal ambivert would, in theory, act as a chameleon, perfectly assuming both introverted and extroverted practices on command. Perhaps, this individual is one whom we could measure and study to cement some neuroscience behind the concept. However, the predominance of public awareness regarding introverts and extroverts (and the associated lack thereof for ambiverts) means that ambivert remains a relatively obscure and unrecognized concept by comparison. Many people do not know what it means to be positioned centrally on the continuum, and thus, they may not know that they are ambiverts.

Participants of experimental studies continue to agglomerate data on introverts and extroverts, causing ambiverts to fall exponentially behind the curve. As a result of an absence of neuroscientific and experimental data, the ambivert remains an understudied concept.

After our introduction to the idea of ambiverts, Karl began mentioning it to executives in his research interviews. When he added this new category, he found that about 20% of executives identified as ambiverts, 40% as introverts, and the remaining 40% as extroverts. Interestingly, this composition differs from an even three-way, 33%, split, as one might expect when there are three available categories.

A remarkable overarching theme presented itself in many of the participants' interviews: at their executive/senior leaders' levels, virtually all interviewees resonated with the importance of balance. Almost all of these business/government/NGO leaders emphasized their efforts to limit the negative impacts of their natural personality type. Additionally, if a situation called for it, they would attempt to assume nondominant traits opposite to their natural personas for the sake of their employees, business partners, or communities at large. If they did not self-identify as ambiverts during the interview, they alluded to their consistent efforts to adopt the ambivert's most important traits.

Assuming that those who self-identified as ambiverts were born as such, how do these natural ambiverts differ from learned ambiverts? In truth, we are not sure. Further research into ambiverts should promote a greater understanding of this demographic, and we hope to solidify the concept as a legitimate area of psychological study, applicable to leadership, management, and a multitude of other areas. From that point, we hope that someday in the future the differences between learned and innate ambiversion may become known.

For our purpose, however, the answer to this question does not matter. Above all, we aim to emphasize the apparent awareness and flexibility common in ambiverts and how these qualities seem to coincide with effective leadership, regardless of whether this ambiversion is inherent or assumed/learned.

In light of this strong trend among business leaders, this book argues that ascension up the corporate/organizational ladder, or success in other forms, requires the flexibility and awareness inherent in the ambiverted nature. Thus, to ensure corporate, academic, or other forms of success, we recommend that one assume the traits of an ambivert and, eventually, become one. We are all ambiverts now, or at least we should be!

Best of Both Worlds

It's not just CEOs who benefit from ambiversion either. In fact, the earlier in your career you build these skills, the better, since the benefits will improve over time. For people who identify as extroverts, this may mean being consciously quieter in meetings; for introverts, it may mean contributing more in meetings.

Alisa Cohn, a startup and CEO coach based in New York City

The ambivert can assume an introverted or extroverted persona with relative ease. Therefore, they are capable of harnessing the strengths of each communication style while avoiding their weaknesses by assuming the opposite traits. As a reminder, the strengths of introverts and extroverts, as explained in the earlier sections of this book, are listed below:

Introvert Strengths	Extrovert Strengths
1. Good listeners.	1. Masters of energy.
2. Reading the room, more valuable contributions to discussions.	2. Masters of the social network.
3. Refined internal processing.	3. Overall confidence.
4. Greater ability for focus, creativity, and development of passion.	4. Motivational speaking, uplifting others.
	5. Taking charge of transformational leadership.

Ambivert Breaks

You know, you've coined this term ambivert and I find it useful. I used to think I was totally an extrovert, and I think I'm kind of swinging toward the middle. Now, I find, you know, a lot of ministers are introverts and I'm not sure that I'm a pure introvert, but I do need that time of recharging away from people, especially because so much of the pastor's life is giving of oneself publicly. I think to balance that kind of giving and to balance the energy of standing in front of a church of five hundred people five times a Sunday.

Cate Anthony (Priest at St. Stephen's Episcopal Church, Richmond, Virginia, USA)

We have mentioned and we will discuss at more length soon, both introvert and extrovert breaks, but what kind of breaks do ambiverts take? Unlike those of introverts and extroverts, our research suggests that the recharging breaks of ambiverts depend on the context of their actions and environment. When an ambivert acts like an extrovert at length, they tend to recharge by acting more introverted; on the other hand, after acting like an introvert for an extended period of time, they tend to take extrovert breaks. So, they take both introvert and extrovert at times, depending on how they have acted prior to the need for the break.

It is important to note here that ambivert breaks are essentially just combinations of introvert and extrovert breaks, as required by the ambivert.

Strengths of Ambiverts

Awareness

> To sit with yourself and be with yourself, learn awareness of your thoughts. Develop the patience to sit with your emotions and not always react. I think it's one of the most powerful tools as an entrepreneur you can have.
>
> David Segal (Co-founder of DAVIDsTEA and now Firebelly
> Tea chain of stores)

The ambivert is acutely aware of themselves, their surroundings, and others in their environment. They observe, process, and internalize information, knowing the appropriate moment to act on this knowledge in order to obtain the best possible outcome. Not only does this practice guide the ambivert in their role as a leader, but it also instils a sense of confidence in those around them. Perhaps this awareness quality is derived from the ambivert's more introverted nature, but it takes on a new light when paired with the adaptability and flexibility of ambivert communication.

Mark Hantho, Vice Chairman of Citigroup Inc., one of the biggest banks in the world, believes that one of the best sources of intel for a leader is the others partaking in a given discussion:

> I benefit greatly from other people's thinking. I really do. And I'm not just saying that because there are some seriously smart people at Citigroup and, you know, again with clients. So I would say that I'm a good listener and then I convert that into an energy that I think is relevant at the right time.

Ambiverts are the best candidates to benefit from others' contributions to group collaboration, as Hantho describes. Like extroverts, ambiverts can encourage discussion in their more reserved colleagues, and like introverts, they can take in this new information and ensure that it is put to good use. Awareness is key in both the introverted and extroverted behaviours involved in this mechanism, so the ambivert is most likely to execute it properly. They are able to use the skills of extroverts and introverts better than extroverts and introverts because of this awareness.

The awareness of introverts can sometimes be rendered less effective by their reluctance to speak up. An introvert might notice that a colleague has something important to say, that the solution proposed in a meeting doesn't fully address the problem, or that the discussion is off track, but they may hesitate to express these observations due to a lack of assertiveness. An ambivert or extrovert, however, is able to maintain a more detached perspective on the situation and speak up when the timing feels right. They are not hesitant to share their viewpoint, especially when they believe it to be constructive.

Furthermore, this skill of awareness extends beyond meetings and social interactions. Due to their keen perception of their surroundings, ambiverts often notice things that extroverts might overlook because of their very outgoing nature. Ambiverts, like extroverts, are less likely than introverts to stay confined to their desks; instead, they observe the flow of the office, ask questions, and listen to the answers, spotting small mistakes or discovering better ways to implement strategies and operations. This awareness also serves as a powerful tool for preventing crises before they occur and for resolving conflicts between employees.

Ultimately, what makes the awareness of ambiverts so effective is their ability, like introverts, to develop a deep understanding of their work environment and to act on that awareness. By doing so, they create unique opportunities and avoid common pitfalls by responding promptly and appropriately.

Flexibility

I am a hybrid extrovert introvert. In terms of leading a company, you need to be loud sometimes. People will look for those cues from you. But you also need the introverted side—you have to contemplate, understand yourself and what you know, in order to have that kind of vision of what the company is, where it is at, and what it is capable of.

John Lomow (CEO and co-founder of agri startup Fieldness)

Ambiverts possess a unique ability to seamlessly switch between extroverted and introverted behaviours, granting them the versatility to adapt to any scenario by effectively utilizing either set of traits as the situation demands.

To illustrate this behaviour in action, consider the following scenario.

Imagine an ambiverted CEO named John stepping into an executive meeting room, wherein he immediately taps into his extroverted side to warmly greet colleagues and engage in friendly small talk, creating a positive team dynamic. This ambivert leader then captures everyone's attention with a charismatic pitch on the pressing need to cut corporate expenses, again leveraging his extroverted side.

Following this successful introduction, John puts on his introvert cloak by engaging in attentive listening. He invites his colleagues to share their thoughts on solving this financial problem, carefully considering each input without interruption. After the meeting, our CEO retreats to his desk and reflects quietly on the team's suggestions. Here, the introverted strength resides in the ability to craft a well-considered strategy built upon the collective insights offered by others.

In this scenario, John's versatility and flexibility enable him to create a successful team environment by equally leveraging his introverted and extroverted sides.

If this exercise seems familiar, it is because we gave a similar example in Chapter 3 to illustrate the importance of striking a balance to best approach the task at hand. The ambivert leverages extroversion by remaining confident through adversity and maintaining an enjoyable and collaborative team dynamic. On the flip side, listening to others instead of expressing an opinion first and reflecting with deep focus leverages introverted qualities to the CEO's advantage. Clearly, the ambivert is best equipped to tailor their behaviour in accordance with the unpredictable and changing circumstances they might be faced with as a leader in today's crazy dynamic world. This instils trust in colleagues and stakeholders that the ambiverted executives can deal with whatever comes their way. Ultimately, flexibility is one of the ambivert's most notable and revered qualities.

Collaboration

> Sometimes you just need to see how it is and make sure that everybody understands where you're going with your plan. But on the other side, you have to be able to listen and you have to be able to take the time to understand, and that's what listening is supposed to be doing, is to help you understand before you can provide guidance or directions. It's important to first understand the problem you're trying to tackle.
>
> General Jenny Carignan (Chief of the Defence Staff of Canada, the most senior general in Canada, who is in charge of the Canadian military)

Ambiverts, with their talent for awareness and adaptability, bring a set of unique qualities that make them effective collaborators. Because they naturally balance listening and talking, they are particularly effective communicators in group settings.[14] This ability to adapt their communication style to meet the needs of different team members allows ambiverts to forge strong connections critical for teamwork.[15]

In today's diverse team environment, wherein innovation, problem-solving and creativity flourish from a mix of ages, ethnicities, genders and educational backgrounds, effective communication is key.[16] Managing this diversity is not just beneficial for organizational performance—it is essential. Ambiverts are particularly adept at navigating the communication hurdles that diversity and the different communication styles and preferences across team members can present. Their balanced approach is highlighted by Adeoye et al. (2023)[17] as instrumental in promoting collaboration among culturally diverse groups. By leveraging their balanced personality for the benefit of team dynamics, ambiverts enhance the group's overall performance.

The positive influence of ambiversion on teamwork can be seen through the lens of social learning theory, which suggests that behaviours and attitudes are learned by observing and mimicking others.[18] Ambiverts, by demonstrating effective communication and collaboration, can serve as exemplary figures within teams. Finally, Adam Grant's 2013 study connects ambiverts' superior sales performance to their versatile personality, suggesting their potential to excel in diverse group collaborations through their capability to connect with a broad spectrum of personalities.[19]

More Effectively Creative Than Introverts

Ambiverts are known to be creatives—another strength derived from their introverted side. In one of my interviews with her, Susan Cain revealed that those who are most successfully creative are often a mix of introverted and extroverted—extroverted enough to exchange ideas with others, yet introverted enough to fully partake in the creative process alone and for long periods.[20] As an ambivert, the ability to openly discuss and share thoughts, and then listen to actor feedback from potentially valuable mentors or related experts, might make the idea and product better than it ever could have been if produced in isolation.

We might venture to say that this trait would make ambiverts the best entrepreneurs as well—they have the endurance to work through an idea alone for as many hours as it takes until it is functional, while maintaining the presentation skills and charisma necessary to show off their idea to investors.

A former student of Karl's and fellow extreme extrovert (mentioned in Chapter 4), Kat Garcia, is now a co-founder of an up-and-coming startup in New York City, Ground. Ground is an AI-powered platform that helps consumer companies grow by scanning and detecting revenue-generating opportunities in the background. In an interview with two of three of the company's co-founders, Garcia shared some tips for surviving and succeeding in the entrepreneurial grind, all of which bode well for demonstrating ambiverted entrepreneurship in action.

Hard work is a necessary factor for startup success, although not sufficient on its own. Garcia recommends constant analysis and innovation to combat potential uncertainties. The long hours and the focused passion of an introvert on their projects are a necessity for hard work.

The company has interviewed hundreds of different businesses to consistently adapt their product to changing demands. Especially as an entrepreneur in technology, it is important to set out predictions and scenarios for the future—this process transforms abstract ideas into realistic possibilities, bringing your concepts to life. In addition, the Ground's co-founders appreciate the power of the social network, as it provides vital support to propel the startup forward. Both of these tips require the vivaciousness and consistent sociability of extroverted charm.

Weaknesses of Ambiverts

> I am both. I'm an extrovert and then I freak out and go back to my cave.
> David Bensadoun (CEO at Aldo Group, a global
> shoe retailer of over 20,000 employees)

Although they earn their successes, ambiverts are not perfect—they have their weaknesses too. We have identified two potential shortcomings of the moderate position. First, ambiverts are at risk of appearing inauthentic. Second, because they are so flexible, ambiverts are unpredictable in their behaviour, making them highly confusing to work with on occasion.

During a memorable trip to Japan and Thailand with undergraduate students, I encountered a situation that encapsulates the challenges faced by ambiverts. One evening, I found myself sitting alone in the lobby of our hotel, deep in thought. My solitude was not borne out of illness or discomfort, it was only a result of jet lag.

However, this act of seeking solitude led to a series of inquiries from several students, all of whom were concerned about my well-being. They assumed that my decision to be alone was indicative of feeling unwell. Their misconception highlights a common challenge for ambiverts: the difficulty in being understood by others, which might cause suspicions of inauthenticity or confusion.

Inauthenticity

> Am I an introvert? Am I an extrovert? How does that affect my leadership style? And
> just an awareness that you shouldn't try to be somebody you're not.
> Adam Bryant (the Corner Office columnist of the *New York Times* for over a
> decade, a journalist who has interviewed hundreds of CEOs)

We face a problem of inauthenticity in today's society. We have access to unlimited amounts of information, yet no efficient vehicle to sort this data and identify accurate information from data that is misleading, incorrect, or useless. This issue of truth has seeped into the realm of leadership, and authenticity has thus become a crucial focus in management. Companies, employees, and citizens in general are searching for authentic CEOs to lead their companies honestly, pro-actively, and with pure intention.

Although ambiverts are versatile and can take on many different roles within a company, Ankeny argues that because they wear many hats, ambiversion can be seen as inauthentic when leaders change their management style for different employees.[21] By nature, ambiverts adjust their behaviour based on circumstance, oscillating between introversion and extroversion as the situation demands. This adaptability, although a strength in most contexts, can sometimes be misunderstood as a lack of genuine personality. The ambivert's ability to modulate their engagement level by being more reserved in some situations and outgoing in others might lead observers to question their authenticity. While this ability to adapt to different situations can be a strength, it can be challenging to understand the true personality of an ambivert, and therefore easy to assume that they are wearing a mask to please others. Even worse, their seamless ability to adjust their behaviour might appear, in some lights, as tactful manipulation to achieve an unknown end goal.

Confusing and Unpredictable Behaviour

My daughter told me I was a chameleon. She said that I adapt.
Christiane Germain (CEO of Groupe Germain Hotels, 23 hotels across Canada and thousands of employees)

Because ambiverts naturally act like introverts in certain cases and extroverts in others, they have a wider variety of potential responses to any given situation. This tends to confuse their subordinates and colleagues as it makes it fairly difficult to predict their behaviour. Although this may prove advantageous in some circumstances, such as in competitive business environments where success is dependent on strategy unforeseen to the opposition, inconsistent behaviour within a team often creates opportunities for frustration, discord, and conflict.

In team settings, the unpredictable nature of ambiverts can lead to confusion among team members who may struggle to anticipate their responses or preferences. This uncertainty can complicate decision-making processes, project planning, and the establishment of consistent team dynamics. A leader has to be aware of this shortcoming to keep their team in alignment and minimize conflict or confusion.

For ambiverts in leadership positions, the fluctuation between assertiveness and receptiveness might confuse subordinates as regards to expectations and leadership style. Although flexibility in leadership is often valued, excessive unpredictability can hinder the development of a clear and cohesive vision, which might in turn affect team morale and efficiency.

Our Key Takeaways

#1 The ambivert is successful because they emulate emergent strategy in the contexts of leadership and communication.

A greater focus on learning and deliberate adaptation is related to the growth mindset introduced in previous chapters. The ambivert's flexibility in response to various circumstances of their environment, in combination with their greater awareness of their surroundings, allows them to detect the need for change in their approach and follow through on this change. Their introverted and extroverted qualities result in a stronger ability to *strike a balance* and create a more resilient strategy, which survives and adapts to internal and external expectations that are placed on the executive.

#2 The ambivert's strength is that she/he is the best of both worlds. Their weaknesses stem from others' misunderstanding their behaviour.

The ambivert is aware of themselves, their surroundings, and others in their environment. They know when to take action regarding knowledge gained from this awareness exercise, and they are capable of harnessing the strengths of introverts and extroverts while avoiding their weaknesses. This overall flexibility and awareness coincide with effective leadership. Despite this versatility, the ambivert is at risk of appearing inauthentic. They are also sometimes difficult to work with, as their actions are unpredictable and confusing.

#3 Ambiverts need breaks, too.

They are not superheroes. How the ambivert recharges depends on the context of their actions and environment. This break could take the form of introvert or extrovert breaks, depending on which scenario they have been excessively exposed to in the recent past.

Notes

1 Evans, Richard I., Jung, Carl, and Jones, Ernest. *Conversations with Carl Jung and Reactions from Ernest Jones*. Princeton, NJ: D. Van Nostrand Company, 1964. A transcript of the authors filmed interviews with Dr. Carl Jung before his death. Presents a lucid presentation of Jung's fundamental concepts and comments on common psychological topics, with comments from Dr. Ernest Jones.
2 Petric, Domina. "The Introvert-Ambivert-Extrovert Spectrum." *Open Journal of Medical Psychology* 11, no. 3 (2022): 103–111. https://doi.org/10.4236/ojmp.2022.113008. Investigates the spectrum of personality and introduces the term of ambiversion using literature, author's experiences and reflections. Finds

that life energy, referred to as "libido," has direction which characterises the nature of one's personality; it is possible to train the mind to adopt habits of the other extreme.

3 Patel, Vipul B. "Five Factor Personality Model of Leadership." *International Journal of Research in Humanities and Social Sciences* 2 (2014). Establishes five major, dominant personality traits that will emerge at one of three levels.

4 Petric, Domina. (2022).

5 Conklin, E. "The Definition of Introversion, Extroversion and Allied Concepts." *The Journal of Abnormal Psychology and Social Psychology* 17, no. 4 (1923): 367–382. https://doi.org/10.1037/h0065888.

6 Davidson, Ian J. "The Ambivert: A Failed Attempt at a Normal Personality." *Journal of the History of the Behavioral Sciences* 53, no. 4 (2017): 313–331. https://doi.org/10.1002/jhbs.21868.

7 Grant, Adam M. "Rethinking the Extraverted Sales Ideal." *Psychological Science* 24, no. 6 (2013): 1024–1030. https://doi.org/10.1177/0956797612463706.

8 Fudge, C. "The Five Factor Model of Personality and Sales Performance." *Journal of Individual Differences* 29, no. 1 (2008): 11–16. https://doi.org/10.1027/1614-0001.29.1.11.

9 Mintzberg, Henry and Waters, James A. "Of Strategies, Deliberate and Emergent." *Strategic Management Journal* 6 (1985): 257–272. Relating issues in strategic choice to real-world strategies elaborating on existing strategies uncovered in research.

10 Mintzberg, Henry and Waters, James A. (1985). Porter identifies five forces that determine competition within an industry: the threat of new entrants, bargaining power of suppliers, bargaining power of buyers, the threat of substitute products or services, and rivalry among existing competitors. See Porter, Michael E. "How Competitive Forces Shape Strategy." *Harvard Business Review* 57 (1979): 137–145.

11 Porter identifies five forces that determine competition within an industry: the threat of new entrants, bargaining power of suppliers, bargaining power of buyers, the threat of substitute products or services, and rivalry among existing competitors. See Porter, Michael E. (1979).

12 The five segments of technology adopters are: Innovators, Early Adopters, Early Majority, Late Majority, and Laggards. See Moore, Geoffrey A. *Crossing the Chasm: Marketing and Selling High-Tech Products to Mainstream Customers.* New York: Harper Business, 1991.

13 Mintzberg, Henry and Waters, James A. (1985): 257–272.

14 Kim, K. H., Oh, H., and Kim, Y. J. "The Role of Ambiversion in Cross-Cultural Collaboration: A Dyadic Perspective." *Journal of Business Research* 131 (2021): 168–177.

15 Castaner, Xavier and Oliveira, Nelson. "Collaboration, Coordination, and Cooperation Among Organizations: Establishing the Distinctive Meanings of These Terms Through a Systematic Literature Review." *Journal of Management* 46, no. 1 (2020): 965–1001. https://journals.sagepub.com/doi/10.1177/0149206320901565.

16 Turi, J. A., et al. "Diversity Impact on Organizational Performance: Moderating and Mediating Role of Diversity Beliefs and Leadership Expertise." *PLoS One* 17, no. 7 (2022).

17 Adeoye, Moses Adeleke. "Impact of Ambiversion on Collaboration Among Diverse Groups." *Jurnal Pedagogi dan Pembelajaran* 6, no. 2 (2023): 226–230.

18 Bandura, Albert and McClelland, David. *Social Learning Theory.* 1st ed. Englewood Cliffs, NJ: Prentice Hall, 1977.

19 Grant, Adam M. (2013).

20 Moore, Karl. "Susan Cain: 'Introverted Leaders Often Deliver Better Outcomes than Extroverted Leaders'." *Financial Post*, February 9, 2016. https://financialpost.com/executive/leadership/susan-cain-introverted-leaders-often-deliver-better-outcomes.
21 Ankeny, Jason. "A Winning Personality: Why Ambiverts Make Great Entrepreneurs." *Entrepreneur*, March 5, 2015. https://www.entrepreneur.com/article/242502.

Chapter 6

The Introspective Extrovert

> As I get more senior, I must listen more and talk less. I know what I know already, and I want to learn from others in order to create a better strategy.
>
> Zoe Yujnovich (EVP of Shell)

In the introduction, we told the story of an introverted CEO managing a major multinational. In my CEO Insights class, Claude Mongeau explained that he had to put on his "game face" whenever he left his floor in order to act like an extrovert if necessary. Much of management leadership academia today is dedicated to identifying recommendations for introverts like Mongeau to cultivate such a game face. A topic less approached by my colleagues, however, is the other side of the coin—extroverts like myself must also put on their "game face" and act like introverts at times. What is good for the goose is good for the gander.

Part of senior management's job is to see innovation within the organization and to have the good judgement to fund and resource the innovative solutions that possess the most traction. In the face of great uncertainty during the COVID pandemic, this particular role requirement of the executive grew to a larger level than ever before. In alignment with the increasingly turbulent environment of many industries experiencing revolutionary new trends in the workforce, we must pick up the pace of change within our firms. A key way to effectively remain aligned is going to be boundary-spanning employees, with one foot in the customers/suppliers/partners world, and the other inside the firm. Learning is becoming more important than dominance. Introverted strengths—their willingness to listen, taking the time to do appropriate analysis before making decisions, and putting others front and centre in the spotlight—are especially useful here. For the extrovert, the challenge is to play the part of the introvert: to listen carefully and analytically and to work with the team to figure out the appropriate way forward in uncertain situations.

DOI: 10.4324/9781003612216-7

Introverted and Extroverted Clergy

Karl has interviewed a number of clergy about how they must act like an extrovert after giving an inspiring (hopefully) message in services. He interviewed a Catholic priest, a Church of Iceland priest, two Jewish rabbis, three Protestant pastors and two Imams. A common thread ran through what they said. They worked hard to develop a spiritually inspiring message for Friday, Saturday, or Sunday religious services. This was seen as a more typically introverted activity, all spent hours looking over holy texts, commentaries and other books, reflecting on the profound truth of the message they were trying to share. Giving the message took considerable energy as they sought to lift up, encourage and inspire the members of their congregations. After this considerable effort, in all cases, they were expected to go and talk to the members of their group. Members were often quite eager to thank them, to comment on the message and at times argue a bit with what they said. They were required to act more like an extrovert in order to be an effective and appropriate clergy member. Though for the introverts, it was made easier because it was often more one-on-one or one on two. The Icelandic priest told me that he could excuse himself from coffee after 30 minutes or so and go recharge in his office, the others were more typically spending 45 minutes to an hour. Which made it easier for the introverts. For the extroverts, it was more natural to talk to members, sometimes for an hour or two. The challenge for more extroverted members of the clergy was the hours in their studies preparing the messages.

This chapter aims to offer tangible advice that readers may use to tackle their natural predisposition towards extroverted weaknesses without restricting the power of their capabilities. As an extroverted leader, Karl believes he has grown as a leader by learning to emulate the strengths that many introverted or quiet leaders bring to the table. We hope to pass on these learnings to you.

The Extrovert Managing Themselves and Other Extroverts More Effectively

Listen More, Talk Less

> I'm a big extrovert. But over the years, we also learned that there are introverted moments that are important for you and for others. Asking questions is very important. Right. And many times, just listening. Be a good listener.
>
> Francisco Salazar (Global leader at Monitor Deloitte)

Listen more, talk less is a critical lesson for extroverts—we cannot stress this enough. Opening one's ears to the conversation increases their chances of learning from others and identifying new points of information that could be strategically advantageous. Conversely, the extroverted mindset's occupation with active engagement with their surroundings is likely to result in domination or excess verbal participation in discussions. This approach often leads to less learning and informed strategic decision-making.

One way that extroverts can ensure they are actively listening and learning during meetings is by asking questions. Posing well-thought-out questions offers an opportunity for the extrovert to engage with their surroundings as they prefer, while simultaneously increasing the extrovert's capacity to hear and understand the opinions of those around them.

Many politicians, like Jean Charest, for example, who was the Premier of Québec and the head of the Federal Conservative Party of Canada in Ottawa, talk about the need for the extroverted political/government leader to be an excellent listener as central to what they must do. Karl asked Jean about how he ran cabinet meetings as the Premier of Québec, and how he worked with the deputy ministers, who are the senior members of the governmental bureaucracy that are central advisers to the Premier and cabinet ministers. Particularly with the deputy ministers, you must listen very carefully and at length, Jean stressed. We have also heard this from a number of other current and former senior leaders. Deputy ministers are at the pinnacle of the bureaucracy, so they are very talented people, but also often have spent years involved in the issues that the Premier is trying to decide on. They and their staff know much more than you do, and so you need to listen and generally follow their advice. Political realities may occasionally affect the officials, but this is often an unwise option.

Melanie Joly, the Canadian Foreign Minister, told Karl that as she goes around the world representing Canada, she must listen to the local people, starting with the Canadian ambassador, in order to approach her counterparts and other senior leaders in the country she is visiting in order to be effective. The ambassador is much more in touch with the issues on the ground in that country and acts as an adviser she simply must listen to.

Productivity and leadership evangelist Pierre Khawand adopted the "Be Silent" break from a mindfulness book by Jon Kabat-Zinn.[1] Instead of using this method during meditation, however, he recommends it for the workplace. Although it might seem like an extrovert break, it is not. Furthermore, it is a great in-the-moment strategy to promote listening to and awareness of others.

The "Be Silent" break is a moment taken by extroverts to focus conscious attention, first on their surroundings and then on themselves. Initially, this includes the emotions of the people around you, their body language, or any hidden cues that might have been previously missed. Afterward, the extrovert should direct their consciousness inwards, paying attention to the feelings or instincts arising in response to what was observed externally. Mindfulness and meditation could be used as a formidable strategy for extroverts to employ better listening and awareness of their surroundings. A number of CEOs have mentioned it on the CEO Series show or the CEO Insights MBA class. Keeping physical shape has been something that Karl has been asking CEOs about for over a decade, but since COVID, he has also been asking about mental health. As we mentioned earlier, meditation is an approach that many CEOs have adopted since COVID.

Here are several examples from CEOs of some pretty big companies:

In March 2024 Karl visited the American University in Cairo, as part of the visit he interviewed on stage in front of hundreds of their alumni, Marwa Abbas who is the General Manager and Technology Leader of IBM Egypt. She spoke about her habit of meditating,

> I always like to have my 'me time' in the morning. So even if I leave at seven, I, wake up at five, and I have two hours of what you can call meditation. I pray and I sit with myself. This is something I never compromise, this is the one thing I'm very strict on.

Jean-Christophe Bedos is the CEO of Birks, a chain of 28 high-end jewelry stores across Canada. He spoke about his habit of regular meditation,

> It is a moment of connection between the brain and the heart, where it's a very short five, six minutes meditation, where you connect your breathing with the rhythm of your heart. You do that two or three times a day. And I can tell you, this is an incredible, very powerful solution that doesn't take long. But it does help to cope, especially when you have very stressful moments.

Mairead Lavery is the CEO of EDC, an over 2,000-employee organization EDC is Canada's trade finance agency that helps Canadian firms export around the world. She told Karl,

> Recently I've started back on meditation, and I had started this practice a number of years ago and I really had sort of lost my way in terms of meditation but returned to it. I've been meditating again, it helps me calm my thoughts. I do find it very helpful.

Alexis Smirnoff, CTO and CO-Founder at Dialogue, a Canadian telemedicine firm that competes globally and the number one provider in Canada, was recently acquitted by financial services giant Sun Life, "I stay active like that, you know, skiing and mental health. I have also tried for quite an extensive period of time meditating."

Emily Heitman, Country President, Canada at Schneider Electric, a French industrial technology leader with over 168,000 employees worldwide told Karl this about meditation,

> Everybody's wired differently. I can't prescribe for somebody how to check out, and how to make time for themselves. For me, what works is that I'm a

big fan of meditation. I practice it in the morning before I get out of my home and go to the office to regulate my perspective on life.

Mindfulness and meditation are becoming increasingly popular in the corporate world, especially among leaders who seek to improve focus, resilience, and mental clarity. Introducing mindfulness practices in the workplace reflects a broader corporate response to the rising demand for mental health support and stress management. Many prominent executives have incorporated meditation into their daily routines as a way to enhance their performance and maintain balance in high-stress environments.

For instance, Oprah Winfrey dedicates 20 minutes a day to meditation, while Bill Gates and Jeff Weiner, the former CEO of LinkedIn, also incorporate mindfulness into their busy schedules. Ray Dalio, founder of Bridgewater Associates, has been practicing Transcendental Meditation for over 45 years, attributing much of his success to this regular practice. Bill Ford, Executive Chairman of Ford Motor Company, has even integrated mindfulness into Ford's corporate culture, offering meditation sessions and yoga classes. Reflecting on the evolution of corporate culture, Ford noted, "Our executives all had foot-long cigars back in the day and their stomachs hanging out like this and, you know, two-martini lunches. It's a very, very different culture."[2]

These examples illustrate how mindfulness practices, such as the "Be Silent" break suggested by Pierre Khawand, can foster a more mindful and attentive workplace. For extroverted leaders, incorporating moments of silence and reflection can be an effective strategy to enhance listening, tune into subtle social cues, and develop greater awareness of both their own responses and the emotions of those around them.

Mindfulness brings about various positive psychological effects, including increased subjective well-being, reduced psychological symptoms and emotional reactivity, and improved behavioral regulation.[3]

Mindfulness has been theoretically and empirically associated with psychological well-being. The elements of mindfulness, namely awareness and nonjudgmental acceptance of one's moment-to-moment experience, are regarded as potentially effective antidotes against common forms of psychological distress—rumination, anxiety, worry, fear, anger, and so on—many of which involve the maladaptive tendencies to avoid, suppress, or over-engage with one's distressing thoughts and emotions.

Build Genuine Connections With Others

I am completely on the extrovert side. Some would even refer to me. Some have referred to me as a power extrovert. I get all of my energy being around other people.

So I'm very much. I think there are some tasks that require my full attention, that require my entire capacity, and for those I need the least amount of distraction as possible. But when I want to relax or I want to unwind after a tough day or a tough week or a tough month, it is with people. It's with people that I like and respect. . . . I enjoy taking a walk by myself and listening to a podcast or reading a book. But the way that I really relax is being around other people.

Harley Finklestein (President of Shopify)

Due to their charisma and social ability, the extrovert usually maintains a large web of acquaintances, often because these are helpful for strategic, personal, or business objectives. Unfortunately, however, it is difficult to hold strong ties with and remain genuine to so many people at once. Therefore, the extrovert sometimes experiences problems with authenticity.[4] Since the culture of personality's problem of anonymity has shifted to one of authenticity, such a personality flaw is fatal—the extrovert is at risk of appearing to be contributing to this issue for society at large.

If the extrovert wishes to mitigate this concern and reap the benefits associated with the skills of introverts, one way to do so is to emulate the introverted practice of creating close friendships. This is not to say that the extrovert must abandon their large network in favour of a much smaller circle of constituents—it is not their style anyway. Rather, the practice of building close friendships with genuine effort (genuine being the key word here) and caring about these friends should be applied at a reasonable scale to the extrovert's network.

An objective of genuine connection requires a greater understanding of one's friends, which, in turn, can be achieved through learning about them by listening to what they emphasize during conversations (yet another demonstration of the "listening more" strategy).

Using available information to make others feel heard is a sure way to increase the strength of one's interpersonal bonds. It really is the simple things that make the difference here. For example, making someone feel heard might look like taking care to pay attention to the subjects of small talk, such as a particular sports game or news headline, and then returning to them with greater knowledge, research or an opinion to further discuss.

Another go-to strategy is making notes of your peers'/subordinates' birthdays and ensuring that you congratulate them on another year when the day comes around—a small gesture, but an important one nonetheless, to demonstrate that they are valued. Paul Demarais III, CEO at Sagard Holdings, taught Karl this one: he takes the time to wish every one of his Facebook friends well on their special day.

As a secondary function, the extrovert should consider building a smaller social group of trusted partners of their own. This practice has proven to be extremely beneficial to the mental health of those who adopt it. Studies show that the introvert is more selective in establishing individual relationships—these bonds exhibit much higher levels of empathy than any relationships possessed by the extrovert and are direct producers of greater happiness.[5] The pandemic, by presenting a scenario in which extroverts had to focus on a smaller quantity of relationships, provided the opportunity to cultivate closer and more authentic bonds. Perhaps, during this time, they learned the benefits of having their own tight-knit circles of trust.

Delay Contributions During Group Meetings

> As an extrovert, I actually envy introverts because they would be more expected to reflect on what is being asked of them. Whereas I am pummeled all the time, people expect a quick answer–and that is my style. So I give a fast answer. But at the end of the day, I wonder whether I would have said that differently if I had just calmed down.
>
> Pino Di Ioia (CEO of BeaverTails)

Extroverts should consider sharing their ideas much later in the process of a meeting. Two benefits can be accrued from this. As a senior person, my ideas will too often tend to freeze out others' contributions. Following the good example of introverts, extroverts should delay putting out their ideas until others have had the chance to present theirs. As senior people, we get to decide the forward strategy. We already know our own ideas, so we should make sure that we fully listen to the ideas of others in the most encouraging environment possible: holding off on expressing our opinions is one way to do just that. The second benefit is that our ideas will improve if we have a chance to reflect on them in the course of a meeting rather than blurt them out at the outset. Building on our initial thoughts using the helpful points made by our colleagues will almost always result in a superior idea.

One executive who has taken intentional care to watch the timing of their contributions is David Bensadoun, chief executive of the Aldo Group—the global shoe company headquartered in Montréal—and the son of the company's founder, Aldo Bensadoun. David describes how, when he attends meetings wherein he wants a substantive discussion, he has learned to be quiet and listen to what everyone else has to say before he speaks. If he speaks first, it tends to stall all discussion as the team is intimidated by the presence of the chief executive.

Many of the other executives Karl spoke to agree with this strategy. Like Bensadoun, they will listen to everyone else's ideas first, holding off until the end of the meeting to summarize what the others have said, add their ideas (which have evolved during the meeting thanks to others' proposals), and suggest what the next move for the company should be—which is, of course, the advantage of being the chief executive. Thus, they are tapping into their inner introvert to learn from others and adjust their opinions if necessary before initiating their final say.

Turn the Spotlight Off of Yourself and Onto Others

I had to appoint somebody to do the job that I used to do, and I had to recognize that having appointed that person, I needed to stand back and let him make his decisions. Difficult to do, but you know, if you're not prepared to work with others and to give them scope to develop and to make their own mistakes and learn from their mistakes, well, then you're never going to get the best out of people. I think any extrovert if they're going to be good in leadership, working with teams, you have to be prepared to listen as well as speak.

Willie Walsh (Director General of the International
Air Transport Association)

Extroverts don't mind being the centre of attention—in fact, we rather enjoy it. However, as extroverts progress in their career, they must learn to turn the spotlight away from themselves and beam it onto the people who work for them. It is a necessary part of going from being a star performer to being a manager; *from me to we.*

Directing a collective focus comes naturally for introverts in comparison to extroverts, but it is something my younger employees need and sometimes crave. We must give it to them. It is crucial to keep in mind that extrovert commanders are required to make space and energy for other people, especially introverts, to express themselves and to create a safe space where everyone, regardless of personality type, will feel fully comfortable sharing their own thoughts. As extroverts, these commanders are in the best position to accomplish this objective, even though such an action is more in the nature of the introvert.

As extroverted leaders, we must not only keep our own dominance in check but must further remain vigilant of and discourage other loud personalities from consistently taking over team meetings and discussions. Such a scenario has the same effect on other team members, especially introverted ones, as when we ourselves get excited and hijack the discussion. Although we do not intend to cause harm, these actions will reduce the participation of others and decrease the quality of the final product. We must take care to remind ourselves and others similar to us of the importance of sharing the spotlight. In order to explain to the extrovert's extroverted peers how one might share the spotlight, it might be beneficial to suggest that they, too, follow strategies numbers 1, 2, and 3 in order to ensure that they do not unintentionally take over meetings by asserting dominance over those quieter than they are.

Take Extrovert Breaks!

For example, I'm not very good at cocktails, big parties, or small talk with a lot of people. I'm not good at that. I still read a lot and enjoy taking my time quietly. Yes, I am an extrovert by nature and get a lot of energy from others, but I also take time to reflect.

John McCall MacBain (Canadian billionaire businessman and founder of the
McCall MacBain Foundation and Chancellor of McGill University)

For an extrovert, it is exhausting to shut up and listen—to resist the urge to jump in with ideas and allow others to share the spotlight. Sarah Davis, president of Canadian supermarket giant Loblaw, is another extroverted leader. After the somewhat unnatural act (for her) of being an introvert, she takes "extrovert breaks." This is a newer term in management leadership literature, but it refers to an activity that is the diametric opposite of introvert breaks.

As an extrovert, I have realized that I often take extrovert breaks myself.[6] After sitting and writing alone in my office for a couple of hours, I can't take it anymore: I have depleted my emotional battery by having too much quiet time and a lack of company, and I need to actively seek out stimulation. In fact, perhaps the central point of differentiation between introverts and extroverts is their response to stimulation. Extroverts seek stimulation: it lights up our brains, providing endorphins. Thus, after a few hours of acting like an introvert, I leave my office and head over to the student lounge and group work area, where there are dozens of undergrads who are generally happy to converse with a professor.

Several of my students have shared that they use this approach without even knowing it. Many students frequent the library with their peers to study in a quiet atmosphere, yet will occasionally engage in brief conversational breaks or spontaneous exchanges upon encountering a friend in the library's corridors—both of which would be considered extrovert breaks.

Similarly, when I travel without my wife and children, I generally choose to eat at the bar rather than at a table by myself. I happily talk to total strangers: I find it stimulating and often learn a great deal about the city I am visiting. It's just more fun to me than being by myself. Of course, introverts may shake their heads: after a busy day of meeting new people, they may feel as though there is nothing they would rather do than unwind alone with a restorative meal and a good book. It might even feel better for them to get room service than be in the lobby restaurant.

The benefit of extrovert breaks is a recharge. After spending too long in an unnatural state, it is important to give oneself the opportunity to temporarily return to a preferred state to rest. Routine extrovert breaks allow the extrovert to behave at their best in the moments when performance is most crucial. Thus, it is vital that as a leader, one monitors oneself and their energy levels and takes extrovert breaks as needed in order to always operate at their best. It is also important to keep an eye out for fellow extroverts on the team and ensure that they, too, are not spending too much time alone at their desk, as it is sure to hinder performance and increase the frustration of the overworked individual.

Keeping variety in extroverted breaks is the most effective approach—it will ease the extrovert's dopamine cravings and need for new and stimulating experiences. Need some ideas? Some examples are given below:

Ideas for Extrovert Breaks

- A coffee break with coworkers, or even a simple chat at the water cooler or fountain.

- A short stroll around the office, chatting with people. This might well make you a more popular manager or fellow worker, depending on whom you are talking to.
- Phoning home to speak with loved ones.
- Group collaboration on a relevant issue rather than sitting and thinking by yourself.
- A social dinner or group activities (beer league baseball after work, anyone?).
- Go to a local coffee shop and talk to fellow regulars.
- Take a yoga or other exercise class so you get to connect with your fellow yoga or fitness fans.
- Go and watch a game at a local bar with fellow fans rather than in your basement by yourself.

The Extrovert Managing Introverts

Yes, my boss is an introvert. I scare him, by the way. I've had to change my communication style.

Kim Keating (Board Director, remuneration and nomination committees at Drax Group | previously CCO at Cahill Group Newfoundland)

As the louder, often more aggressive archetype, the extrovert might intimidate the introvert—especially if the latter is timid and shy. Thus, as an extroverted leader, it is all the more important to remain aware of your behaviour, its effects on others, and how to make introverted employees feel safe, comfortable, and ready to contribute. How exactly can you earn their trust? Look below.

Give Them Time to Think and Commit

In the valley, I realized that some of the brightest minds are introverts, and you need patience to understand them. Taking the time to listen to those who may not be outgoing or articulate can give you a superpower, as introverted minds process ideas differently than extroverted ones. My close relationship with my co-founder and my fiancée has taught me to leverage the best of both worlds. Many introverts train themselves to be strong in crowds and effective at public speaking, often appearing extroverted but actually being introverts.

Daniel Saks (co-founder of AppDirect, one of Silicon Valley's most important high-tech firms)

Introverts process internally and need time to do so. It is important to remember that they are not like extroverts—when rushed to process and make a decision aloud, they will freeze. They need the opportunity to be able to think things through and come to conclusions on their own before coming back to the group. As an extroverted leader, it is important to give introverts these opportunities to evaluate the situation. Awareness and sensitivity to their needs are vital for effective leadership of introverts.

Kal Joffres, CEO and co-founder of Tandemic, an Asia-based innovation firm in Singapore, Malaysia, Thailand, and the Philippines, employs a useful strategy to allow introverted employees their special time: "The best way to brainstorm is first to get people to reflect individually and to write things down. Then on the basis of what's written down, start having engagement and discussion." This tactic ensures that the introverts can organize and process all of their thoughts and opinions, allowing them to be ready to participate with valuable contributions.

As an added benefit, this practice forces the extroverts in the room to rehearse the more introverted habit of internal processing. Putting their thoughts on paper can be viewed, in this context, as a method of becoming more internalized in thinking practices.

Prepare a Meeting Agenda and Materials to Pre-Read

I get my energy from reflection and planning. I love being out with people but I find it pretty tiring. I was a diabolical public speaker till my brother asked me to be the best man at his wedding. I learned that public speaking is simply like a conversation as you and I are talking one-on-one today. I try to talk one-on-one whether the audience is 100 or 1000. That's the way that I deliver myself as an introvert. To me, it's not about introversion or extroversion, it's about authenticity and a voice that you use and how that resonates well.

Ed Sims (former Chief Executive Officer at WestJet,
the 2nd largest airline in Canada)

The introvert will appreciate the opportunity to prepare for group environments. If I can let introverts know ahead of time what we are going to be talking about by means of a meeting agenda and reading materials, they can prepare their thinking and do any analysis they feel is appropriate prior to the meeting time and will thus attend the conversation with coherent ideas that have been carefully thought through. Knowing what they are going into and what is expected of them prior to the meeting will allow them to mentally prepare their thoughts and opinions for the conversation to be held. As extroverts, we must understand how introverts approach assignments and give them room to be themselves. Overall, it makes for a more insightful and interesting conversation when introverts and extroverts are both given the resources they need to succeed.

Pro tip: prior to the group meeting, individually approach introverted team members and ask them their opinions. This way, if one of them brings up something you think is of particular importance, you may ask their permission to call on them during the meeting to ensure that the conversation point comes up for discussion. Make sure to get their consent on this before asking them in front of others, as extreme introverts often do not enjoy receiving a cold call.

Do Not Pressure Them to Be at the Front—But If They Want to Be at the Front, Support Them

I've also one last trick: I have a bunch of friends who are extroverts, and I have people who have worked with me that were extroverts because I find it very good for me if I'm working through a room to be with someone who is much more extroverted than me. They will pull me out when I host dinners in Afghanistan for Afghan leaders. I would typically bring one of my extroverted staff members to these small dinners every three or four of us because otherwise, I might clam up at dinner and not say anything. And that person would know that and, you know, pull the conversation off. I think looking didn't work as well for me to walk up to people and offer a picture with me, but I'm really robust and very much a general.

General Stanley McChrystal (retired US four-star general, one of the most senior generals in the world)

The introvert is often not as comfortable as the extrovert in the public eye—it is important to remain aware of this fact. Although it can be productive for leaders to push others out of their comfort zone, this is not always the case. Introverts may prefer to participate in supporting roles or in lead positions that are not public-facing. Here, a good leader should know when pushing out of the comfort zone will be beneficial and when this pressure will be ineffective or even harmful to the employee.

One example in which such a push might be beneficial is related to an exception to the general rule that many introverts do not enjoy public speaking, as explained in Chapter 2. If the introverted individual is especially skilled in a particular field, they are often capable of standing in front of a large crowd to explain their expertise on this subject. In this scenario, some pressure from the leader might result in growth for the introvert through forced practice with their extroverted traits.

However, in most cases, the safe bet is to avoid the pressure. If the introvert does want to be at the front leading, it is paramount that the extrovert supports them. Because the latter is in an influential and powerful position to do so, their influence will have a strongly beneficial effect on the introvert's success.

Meet With Introverts One-on-One and in Small Groups

Sitting on a plane and chatting up someone on the plane. . . . I've never done that in my life. I've never made a cold call to someone. But if I have the ability to engage with people then I tend to listen more one-on-one. I'm not shy to speak in front of

a thousand people, it doesn't matter, but I'm not extremely good at walking over
to people.

> Bertrand Cesvest (executive creative director of Psycho
> Bunny and former CEO of Sid Lee, a leading
> global marketing agency)

Introverts may respond better in smaller groups. Making a conversation
one-on-one or even keeping it down to three people is another way of helping
them to be at ease. Adam Bryant (*The ExCo Group, New York Times Corner
Office* columnist for over a decade*)* believes, "they tend to prefer small group
sessions. So rather than doing big jazz hands at the town hall, they prefer to meet
in small groups in their company." Adam Bryant does not prefer this method for
himself, but he remains sensitive to the needs of his team and acts accordingly.

Francoise Lavertu, co-CEO of Desteia (building supply chain artificial intelligence tools), utilizes a strategy focused on small groups to communicate with
her team: "The way I like to structure the work is to have a weekly meeting with
each person and they get to tell me their bullet points."

Karl has used these ideas in his classroom. For example, he will give more
time for people to reflect in small groups, which appeals to introverts. Similarly,
he will give them material to read ahead of time so they feel more comfortable
to comment in the class—because they have done their homework, they feel
prepared to make a real, valuable contribution.

Quiet Feedback. Do Not Embarrass Them, Even With Much Praise, in Public

Julia Dhar, is a partner at BCG who leads Boston Consulting Group's BeSmart and
Behavioral Science Lab. In an interview with Karl, she talked about the importance of praise. Two-thirds of people say they would like more praise and appreciation from senior leaders. And so, before we start to talk about, well, do we have
the right resources, and is the strategy correct? Have we put in place the right
metrics and goals? Those are important questions, and those are also the tasks of
leadership. But it might also be worth asking, do we have a system to praise and
appreciate the behaviours that we want to see more of? Because that's clearly what
people are telling you they want. We agree with Julia, but we believe an important
nuance is how you praise extroverts and introverts a bit differently at times.

It also depends on the specific person, so use your best judgement with this
tip. Often introverts prefer feedback—even praise—to be delivered one-on-one
as opposed to in a group setting. Being put under the spotlight against their will
in front of many people can be a source of stress and embarrassment for many
introverts. In contrast to extroverts who generally quite enjoy public praise, lap

it up even, most introverts perhaps a less embarrassing approach. But as Julia points out—praise them!

Balance Social Work Environments With Quiet Ones

> Being introverted does not mean that you're unable to be extroverted, it just means that the way you recharge the batteries is different. Extroverts get energy from people and introverts get energy from nature or from being alone. I spend a lot of my time with people, and I feel pretty extroverted right now.
>
> Dani Reiss (CEO of Canada Goose, a top Canadian clothing brand, well-known around the world in colder countries, at least)

Introverts need their space at work. Social areas are built into the traditional office as a means to promote relationship building, networking, and collaboration between employees to drive company success forward. Aside from one's own office, introverted areas at work are often lacking or nonexistent. Thus, if resources allow for it, creating introvert-friendly environments in the workplace is a good strategy to improve the introverted experience, the quality of introvert breaks, and, consequently, the quality of work output.

Many modern office spaces have done just this, taking into consideration the dynamic needs of their employees. Think of Google, Microsoft, or other tech companies: in addition to ping-pong tables and interactive additions to make the workplace more fun and socially engaging, they also often have quiet reflection rooms or silent pods.

Dr. Jennifer Kahnweiler recommends asking the opinion of introverted employees and what they think might improve the office setup.[7] Hearing it directly from the source makes it easier to select renovations suitable to the space and employees, making the outcome more likely to boost employee morale.

Here are some ideas to make your office more introvert-friendly:

Quiet hours in the morning	Give introverts the time and space necessary to wake up and prepare to face the day. This is not to disallow social interaction altogether, but sometimes loud greetings and banter recounting the weekend or day before can be a distraction—not only for introverts, but for anyone trying to think. Quiet hours in the morning provide the space for introverts to prepare themselves for success in whatever tasks they will face in the day ahead.
DND signs[8]	When in the midst of deep individual work, interruption can deter focus for introverts who are busy thinking things through internally. DND, or "do not disturb," signs make this less likely. However, it is advised to keep an eye

(Continued)

(Continued)

	on those with their DND always on the door handle—the signs are meant to promote productivity, and should not be used as a shield from all human connection.
Avoiding open, vast cubicles in place of small team offices— sometimes![9]	Depending on the field of work, open workspaces promoting sociability between coworkers may be necessarily incorporated into an office space, and for good reason. Team spaces promote collaboration and usually entail better results. However, not every industry requires constant group work. A variety of communication spaces is better than the same one in many forms. Private desk space instead of open cubicle desk space allows introverts the solitary opportunities and breaks from socialization they require to function properly. If this is not feasible in the particular office environment, introverts would benefit from some other quiet work environment to think in private and take introvert breaks as necessary—maybe something like the reading rooms with silent pods found in Google offices.
Leave yourself open to suggestions	Your own introverted employees might have valuable ideas as to how to make the office more comfortable for them. It is best to get them directly from the source! To encourage these individuals to confide in you, make sure to always remain open, welcoming, and non-judgemental. And let me know what they say—introverts often have the best ideas!

Give Them Their Introvert Breaks!

I need to understand that [introverts] sometimes need time to recharge through alone time whereas my recharge time is talking time and it's interacting time and working over time. I figured out that I could be very destructive or disturbing to people if I just kept on interacting when they were in their downtime and so understanding that balance has been an important lever for me to better set the people up around me for success.

Eytan Bensoussan (CEO and co-founder of NorthOne,
a Toronto-based Fin-Tech firm)

Introvert breaks are just as important as extrovert breaks! We will delve more into the specifics of these in the next chapter, but for now, it is important to note that extroverted leaders must ensure that their introverted employees are fully charged from introvert breaks and ready to take on the tasks assigned to them.

Our Key Takeaways

#1 Extroverts can be better leaders by adjusting the corporate environment for introverts, not only through their behaviours, but also through changing procedures and the physical setting itself.

Yes, extroverts can act more like introverts—but executive extroverts can do much more. Because office procedures and environments have systematically been built to promote extroversion, socialization, and coworker interaction, it might be beneficial to "introvertize" some spaces and policies within the office in order to make introverted coworkers feel more at ease.

#2 Listening and greater awareness is the key to ambiversion for extroverts.

Many extroverted weaknesses stem from an excess of focus on their own engagement with their environment in place of passively observing and taking in their surroundings. Listening is the number one strategy extroverts can employ to better improve their awareness skills. It will allow them to actually hear what their colleagues say—it sounds ridiculous, I know, but extreme extroverts truly stand to benefit from the practice of consciously and intentionally listening. Perhaps the "Be Silent" break will help them set meaningful intentions to listen better. The benefits of greater listening and awareness are immeasurable.

#3 Creating a culture of empowerment, with patience and support.

Extroverted leaders shine in the spotlight, but it can be an effective strategy to step back and empower others. As we argued earlier in this book, in a world of emergent strategy, a more turbulent world, a less hierarchical, more inclusive approach is critical. For the extrovert, this means being open to others' ideas and allowing space and time to bring them to the fore. You may still be the boss and have to make the final decisions, but very much believe that those decisions must, in most circumstances, be more informed by people who work for you. Let them.

Notes

1 Khanwand, P. "To 'Be' or 'Be Silent': Taking Mindful Breaks Can Help Introverts Keep Up and Extroverts Flourish in the Workplace." *LinkedIn*, 2018.
2 Howard, Phoebe Wall. "Bill Ford at Detroit Economic Club: Of Change in Auto Industry, Yoga, and 2-Martini Lunches." *Detroit Free Press*, October 31, 2017.
3 Keng, L., Smoski, M. J., and Robins, C. J. "Effects of Mindfulness on Psychological Health: A Review of Empirical Studies." *Clinical Psychology Review* 31, no. 6 (2011): 1041–1056. https://doi.org/10.1016/j.cpr.2011.04.006.

4 Duffy, Kathleen A. and Chartrand, Tanya L. "The Extravert Advantage: How and When Extraverts Build Rapport with Other People." *Psychological Science* 26, no. 11 (2015): 1795–1802. https://doi.org/10.1177/0956797615600890.

5 Hills, Peter and Argyle, Michael. "Happiness, Introversion–Extraversion and Happy Introverts." *Personality and Individual Differences* 30, no. 4 (2001): 595–608.

6 When Karl read the literature there was much on introvert breaks but he could not find anything on extrovert breaks so wrote an article for the Wharton Leadership Digest on the Five Types of Extrovert Breaks *cf*: Moore, Karl. "The Five Types of Extrovert Breaks." *Wharton Leadership Digest.* https://leadershipcenter.wharton.upenn.edu/books/five-types-of-extrovert-breaks/.

7 Kahnweiler, Jennifer. "How to Create Introvert-Friendly Office Spaces." *LinkedIn*, 2020.

8 Kahnweiler, Jennifer. (2020).

9 Kahnweiler, Jennifer. (2020).

Chapter 7

The Alluring Introvert

> From the pure definition of introversion, I am one hundred. I draw my energy entirely from the inside. I'm a limited social battery, and I'm happiest when I come home and I'm literally in the basement–that's my happy spot. But on the other hand, by the nature of what I do for a living, I interact with people a lot. We spend all day, all week, all month interacting with people all the time. So it's a learned skill. I'm a well-trained introvert.
>
> Helge Seetzen (managing partner and CEO at TandemLaunch, an entrepreneurial incubator in Canada)

One evening, back in June 2017, Karl took a walk through the streets of downtown Montréal while on a break from grading papers at his desk. It was the city's most eventful weekend—Formula One was in town for the Montréal Grand Prix.

During this stroll, Karl walked past a woman with her bulldog. Being his extroverted self, and without thinking too much about it, he joked with her, asking, "Who's walking who?" Ironically, Karl later learned that this question was a highly appropriate one—the pooch is a vegan model.[1]

As it turned out, the walker was not actually the owner of the dog. This was Lewis Hamilton's bulldog Roscoe, and the woman was his personal assistant. While chatting with this PA, Karl mentioned the CEO Series radio show, and Lewis's manager, Marc, was contacted. He was kind enough to invite Karl as a guest to the Mercedes paddock to interview Lewis for 15 minutes or so.

As Karl sat waiting in the Mercedes paddock for Lewis and Marc, drinking coffee and enjoying the atmosphere, Karl noticed F1 great Niki Lauda sitting by himself at the next table. Once again, his extroverted nature encouraged him to chat with Mr. Lauda. Karl mentioned to him that, at the time, one of his former MBA students worked as the CFO for Lauda Airlines, which he owned. They had a nice discussion about introversion and extroversion in Formula One, wherein Niki explained that, according to his experience, the great majority of Formula One drivers are introverts by nature. Because he, himself, was one of the greatest and longest tenured drivers in F1 history, he knew many who conformed to the

DOI: 10.4324/9781003612216-8

introverted personality type. A few minutes later, Lewis gave a similar answer—he was also an introvert.

This idea was supported recently when Karl got the opportunity to talk with Jefferson Slack, Managing Director at the Aston Martin F1 team. He gave a great explanation:

> Fernando Alonso started karting when he was three. It is an individual sport by definition. . . . When you get to Formula One, you have a teammate who is your biggest competitor because he is the only one driving the same car. Having grown up playing hockey (Jefferson, that is), you develop skill sets and social skills because you win and lose as a team. In F1, it is not the case. In some ways, you are better off being an introvert. You have to do that to beat your teammate and the other 19 drivers on the grid.

Niki's assertion might be surprising at first, seeing as F1 drivers have become some of the most widely recognized public personas in sport during recent years. However, after second thought, their introversion seems very reasonable. They are expert drivers largely because they have allotted the time and commitment necessary to master the skills vital to the practice. They have spent their entire lives pursuing their passion and have sacrificed what many consider to be a normal adolescence to dedicate time to their sport. Niki explained that most of the current grid, in fact, dislikes the limelight and truly cares only about the racing.

There are two takeaways from this story. The first comes from Karl for extroverts like him:

> my extroverted curiosity and confidence to approach both strangers and well-known individuals I recognize in public has often gotten me a lot further than if I had chosen to play to my quieter side and not chatted with them. To be honest, it has also gotten me into trouble on many, many occasions—but on the positive side, I have learned how to apologize more quickly. Extroversion sometimes has undeniable benefits.

The second takeaway is about the drivers: the fact remains that in the public eye, all Formula One drivers (perhaps with the exception of Kimi Raikkonnen) appear extroverted. Considering all of the events, press conferences, and fan meet-and-greets that they are required to attend, it is easy to reach this conclusion. In addition to the normal PR, after one too many Guess the Driver and Never Have I Ever challenges with each other on *Grill The Grid*, the drivers are bound to become comfortable and gain confidence in front of the camera. Their roles simply require them to, at times, act extroverted. They prove that extroversion is a learned skill that is possible to master given the right circumstances and desire.

If personality is measured along an introvert-extrovert spectrum, it is evident that the kind of introverts who enter extroverted workplaces are not extreme in their tendencies. They inherently trust their own ability to assimilate to such an environment and, at the very least, are up for the challenge and willing to act extroverted from time to time as may be required.

Nevertheless, some capable introverts avoid certain turns in their career path out of fear of facing extroverted obligations. Before saying no to yourself on that sales role because cold calls seem daunting, or deciding that a job in investment banking, marketing, public relations, or any other more seemingly extrovert-saturated field is not well suited to a quiet nature, it is vital to consider the added-value opportunity of introverted strengths. The F1 drivers, for instance, have all learned extroverted skills in order to succeed in the public aspects of their role. The core aspects, however, are driven by their dedication, masterful driving skills, and focused ability, all of which stem from their introverted tendencies. Although this is certainly an exceptional example, F1 is a great lens through which to better understand the dynamics of introversion and extroversion in a workplace environment, as well as the expectations for balancing these traits.

The unique success of introverts is related to their ability to learn and master skills as well as their flexibility, listening, understanding, and formation of deep connections with those around them. These skills are unique in extroverted industries and should not be taken for granted. Instead, they should be used to guide you to the top of any field: a list of strategies to assist you in doing so can be found below.

The Introvert Managing Themselves and Other Introverts More Effectively

Use Your Alter Ego

> I'm not an extrovert, I'm a forced extrovert. I'm not heavily introverted either. It's something I had to learn the first time I ran [for office].
> Marc Garneau (former Minister of Foreign Affairs of Canada, retired Royal Canadian Navy officer and former astronaut)

A study by two academics at the University of Queensland experimented with 612 participants in Australia. The study concluded that introverts who adopt extroverted behaviours can be perceived as more effective leaders by others, as compared to when they act introverted. Importantly, introverts did not experience psychological distress from acting extroverted, contrary to what might be expected. However, extroverts who acted introverted felt less positive and more negative emotions compared to those in the control group. The study suggests that introverts can benefit from adapting their behaviour to fit leadership roles and that this can be less uncomfortable and more beneficial than anticipated.[2]

The culture of personality caters to extroverts, and this fact sometimes deters introverts from taking hold of the spotlight for themselves. The introvert is often hesitant to assume a public-facing role, as they are all too aware of the crowd's watchful eye on their every move.

What is the solution to such unease in public settings? Should you "fake it until you make it?" To combat this stage fright, we recommend the practice of assuming an alter ego. The introvert should summon their inner extrovert to the surface to confront these challenges. This new personality can handle any public circumstances that provoke unease within the introvert. Adopting a new persona—particularly one possessing the opposite communication style—will allow them to separate their own experiences and inner anxieties from those of the person on stage.

Scott McDonald, CEO of Oliver Wyman, a global management consulting firm, has had this experience:

> You go to a networking cocktail party at work or work the whole room and go and talk to everyone. You can train yourself to do that. It does drain a lot of your energy, but it's true. Even as an introvert, it's strangely enjoyable to force yourself to do it and to get around and do it.

This strategy is a mindset shift that has the potential to rapidly increase the introvert's capacity to perform in public. It might be difficult to achieve this shift at first, but once accomplished, it will become a useful tool and highly worthwhile for any extrovert-demanding obligations. In fact, this alter ego should work well beyond public appearances; it should also suffice to deal with any task that is not immediately compatible with the introvert's quiet nature. These potential situations could include difficult conversations with peers or subordinates, maintaining confidence during a motivational speech, or negotiating with competitors. The alter ego will transform any introvert into a well-seasoned expert on public relations, human resources management, and leadership during difficult circumstances. It will also help the introvert practice the management strategies recommended throughout the remainder of this chapter.

> I would say I'm, I would say I'm a learnt to be an extrovert. You know, I would say I'm a natural introvert. I really appreciate my quiet time and my reflection. It's a very noisy world. You know, there's lots going on and there is lots to make sense of. And I'm not somebody who is inherently reactive. I'm sort of somebody who likes to take a big picture approach to things, assess deliberately. I talked to a lot of people and then ultimately the decisions that matter in life. I've got a good friend, and we'll go for walks from time to time. And she spent some time in the corporate world and she said, Omar, you know,

try, try in your life to have your own board of directors, you know, people you value who don't necessarily have the same perspective as you do. In fact, try to find people who have opposite perspectives that you do, but people whose opinions and advice you value and then make your own decision. So after conversations with people whom I trust and whose opinions I value, I would really like to take my time and reflect and assess and just, you know, go for walks or go for a workout or listen to music or, you know, spend time with family. But at the same time, part of the job is, you know, you have to have that element. And I do love people, too. So, you know, I would say I'm quite in between. But if I had to pick a side, I'd say introvert.

Omar Sachedina (CTV News anchor on the national evening news, one of Canada's largest television networks)

Assert Yourself

I'm the person who goes in the room and really doesn't want to talk to people. I don't like rejection and that sort of thing. And so but once I got to a certain rank, I knew that it was my responsibility when I was a battalion commander. And you go in the room and you're the senior guy, you're going to take Colonel. They are just sort of military habits where the junior people aren't going to come up and talk to you. So you got to go talk to them. And so I viewed it as responsibility. I had to go do that. And many times when I got very senior, they've never seen a four-star general before, you know, privates and sergeants, I'd never been up close to one. And so you go in the room so they don't know what to do. And so what I found was you had to get up close and, you know, an hour, you should say, Hey, you want to take pictures? And of course, they want to take a picture with you, and send it back to their parents. But I had to do that. And it was a sense of responsibility. I also found out that once I did that, I really liked the interaction. You know, I really liked the ability to get a little bit deeper with people.

General Stanley A. McChrystal (best known for his command of Joint Special Operations Command (JSOC) from 2003 to 2008, and coauthor of two books on leadership)[3]

What strikes us is that a sense of purpose and having something important/valuable to do in the world allows many of us to assert ourselves because the thing we are serving is simply too important to not assert ourselves in the service of this bigger cause.

Let us quote again Nobel Peace Prize winner Muhammad Yunus. He has come to speak at McGill a few times over the years. Karl had the honour of interviewing him, and Yunus clearly stated he was very much an introvert. Karl, somewhat teasing him, said: "But Muhammad I have seen you work a crowd several times and give more than one inspiring speech to groups of thousands here in Montreal. You, sir, are an extrovert!" He said, no, I am very much an introvert, but by giving a speech and working a room, I can help raise millions of dollars every year to help millions of the poorest women and children on earth, how could I not? Muhammad asserts himself because of the great cause he is serving.

Stop Thinking Too Much and Take the Leap

> It is less about like acting in charge or making decisions and more just about, you know, being confident in the process, being confident in the work that was done and being confident in the people and kind of making sure there's a stable ship and being present and available when we're doing well is the time that I can do the things I'm more comfortable doing, you know, reading, thinking about the future, the next step strategy.
>
> Mark Shapiro (CEO Toronto Blue Jays, one of the Major League Baseball teams and a World Series winner)

Just do it! It is hard to explain this piece of advice. What we want to convey here is best portrayed by the story of Balarama Holness, best-selling author and former mayoral candidate of Montréal. In addition to these accomplishments, Holness is a Grey Cup champion (with the Winnipeg Blue Bombers), a McGill law graduate student, and a marathon runner. Based on the diversity of his accomplishments and the challenges he has had to face to achieve success in each of his chosen arenas, it is clear that Holness loves to place himself in uncertain positions in the name of growth: "You have to take risks and put yourself in high-pressure situations."

Unfamiliar and unpredictable circumstances are part of his comfort zone. Running for mayor was actually a decision in which he decided to take the leap.

Before announcing the founding of his Québec provincial party, Bloc Montréal, Holness had strategic concerns: he would be facing well-established political behemoths and had personal apprehensions related to the mental and emotional toll of jumping into hotly contested elections. For several months, he pondered his decision, clearly putting himself at risk of analysis paralysis. Eventually, to prevent any further excessive thinking, he set aside any apprehensions he had and took the leap into yet another high-pressure situation.

Without a formal press release, guided by his intuition alone, Holness picked up the phone and spoke to a journalist, revealing for the first time—both to himself and the journalist—his plan to announce a new political party at the National Assembly the next day. Backed by a team with a firm commitment to gain more economic and political power in his hometown of Montréal, Holness had neither the time to ponder his choice nor the capacity for self-doubt or uncertainty. It became a matter of working under new pressures to meet the objectives he set for himself.

One of the biggest moments of pressure was a televised debate between myself, Valérie Plante, the mayor of Montreal, and Denis Coderre, the former minister of Immigration," he says. "I felt like I had the city on my back. By channeling the lessons I had learned over the years, from the football field to law school, the debate was effortless. Like my father would say, effortless effort.

Clearly, this tactic has paid off for Holness, who has faced and excelled in challenges on the football field, in academia, in society, and in the political arena alike. "I cannot predict where I will be in five years because I'm always shooting for the stars, always aiming for the top," says Holness, who is constantly looking for his next challenge.

Take a page from his book and just take the leap! You will be better off for it.

Know Your Limits. Take Introvert Breaks!

So how do you do it? Because you're always on stage. You're always on display. And part of their answer is they just muscle through it. I don't think being an introvert is any kind of liability for being a CEO. You just have to be self-aware and figure out ways to get the message across.

Adam Bryant (The ExCo Group, *New York Times* Corner Office columnist for over a decade)

Introverts must take introvert breaks as needed to ensure that they can perform at their best. Michaela Chung, writer and private life coach on introversion, argues that introverts should recognize their diverse needs:

You might have different needs than your extroverted colleagues, so you might not be able to go out as much. You might need to schedule in some more recharge time. You might need to spend your lunch hour alone. Sometimes you just have to know what works for you and not feel guilty about it, because ultimately, if you don't honour your introverted needs, you're not going to get as far as you want to go because you may burn out, you may lose confidence in yourself.

Arguably, introverts require more breaks than extroverts do because introvert breaks are not as commonly structured into the average work day as extrovert breaks are in many industries. Certainly, we see networking cocktail events on the schedule more often than quiet time. Thus, introvert breaks are all the more important to keep track of to ensure that the introverts in the office are getting enough alone time.

As an introverted manager, one must ensure that oneself feels recharged and ready to deal with the tasks of the day. Additionally, it is important to watch out for the introverts of the office and ensure that they, too, are working on a full battery. It is less important for introverts than extroverts to maintain variety in their form of break because they do not necessarily crave the same thrill from new experiences and diverse environments as extroverts do. A superior regimen would involve consistently scheduled introvert breaks that are known to work for the specific individual. Here are some examples:

Reading time	Introverts often enjoy the experience of sitting down to enjoy a good book. This is a great opportunity for them to recharge alone. The benefit here is that they are focused on a relaxing task that is usually unrelated to their work responsibilities, which allows them to truly refresh their mind.
Working alone	All introverts love the time to dive deep into their own work. Dedicating hours in the day for solitary study, research, experimentation, projects, or whatever floats your boat as an introvert will refresh your mind and reset you to deal with the more difficult parts of your work day.
The "Be" Break	We already explained the "Be Silent" break in Chapter 6. Referenced in Pierre Khawand's work, meditation expert and author Jon Kabat-Sinn's "Be Silent" break creates the opportunity for intentional quiet time.[4] This break involves a few minutes focused on non-doing and taking the time to just be, letting all thoughts free to wander. It is a form of meditation that prepares oneself to handle the dynamic environment of the world outside the mind.

As an introvert managing other introverts, one may benefit from the conscious decision to include introvert breaks in the work schedule and to establish office layouts that promote introvert breaks. Introverted managers may also use the tactics listed in the section on Managing Introverts in Chapter 6 to create opportunities that will allow introverts to gather their thoughts and prepare for the demanding environment they will face in the world outside their minds.

The Introvert Managing Extroverts

I would say I'm a learn-to-extrovert. I'm a natural introvert. I really appreciate my quiet time and reflection. It's a very noisy world. You know, there's a lot going on and a lot to make sense of. I'm not somebody who is inherently reactive. I'm sort of somebody who likes to take a big picture approach to things, assess, and deliberate.

Omar Sachedina (Chief Anchor and Senior Editor, CTV National News)

Give Them the Time and Room They Need to "Bounce off the Wall With Ideas"

> I am definitely an introvert, but I think about the introvert versus extrovert discussion a little bit differently. I worked for a gentleman a few years ago who helped frame it up really well. For me, introversion doesn't mean that I don't like talking to people or doing interviews or being in front of an audience. It means that when I need to recharge and when I need to re-energize myself, I need quiet time and the opportunity to think like an extrovert like my former boss likes being in big crowds and high energy. And so that really helped me frame it up. But the introversion that I have helps me be a really good listener and reflector and kind of the ability to join together lots of different opinions and ideas and figure out what a solution needs to be.
>
> Penny Wise (Vice President of 3M Canada)

Thanks to their strong internal processing mechanisms, the introvert is known for their creativity. Beyond the extrovert's abundant energy, this personality type can also be highly creative, albeit in a different way than their introverted counterparts. Extroverts are often at their most creative when talking through their ideas with others.

When Karl wants to be creative, he finds a colleague and kicks around some thoughts with them. Often, many subpar ideas emerge in the conversation, but a few excellent ones also come out of this process. Out of the ten ideas, eight might be embarrassing, but that does not bother the extrovert. It is the one or two excellent ideas that make the 20 minutes of bouncing thoughts off the wall worthwhile.

We extroverts think aloud; we just need an audience. In these moments, extroverts would appreciate the patience of their introverted peers and the necessary time this cycle requires to occur and yield results. The ideas that we produce from our verbal brain dumps will make our introverted managers look good—all they need to do is lean in, trust the process, and watch realizations be made and details finalized into well-thought-out strategies or concepts.

Do not Just Listen, but be an Active, Enthusiastic, and Open-Minded Listener

Listening well is seen as one of the traditional strengths of introverts. Compared to extroverts, this strength is definitely a prominent one. Introverts are much more apt to listen and think before jumping in with their thoughts.

Extroverts like Karl typically think by talking, often to our bosses or employees. They need a greater emotional engagement from listeners when they talk. Whether it is when telling a story, presenting slides in a corporate board room, or putting forward a new idea in a meeting, an introvert needs to respond appropriately to their extroverted energy to be the audience member they need.

To be a better manager, introverts must build on one of their greatest strengths by becoming more explicitly active and engaged listeners—your extroverted colleagues will thank you for this adjustment.

What extroverts typically want from my superiors is for them to listen. By listening, we mean to truly do so with engagement and some degree of enthusiasm—otherwise, an extrovert will feel as though the interaction is lacking an emotional response that they need to feel validated! Showing excitement doesn't always equate to agreement, but it is the reassuring support that we require to continue along their train of thought. The introverted leader should, to an extent, respond to an extrovert's natural enthusiasm—but then should also ask me to go give the idea some more thought, do some research, and then draft up an email to them outlining their proposals. These additional efforts in the process will invariably improve their ideas.

Although introverts are very capable listeners, they tend towards what extroverts identify as passive listening. As an extrovert gets excited, they seek active listening. When a listener sits there—like a *bump on a log* as extroverts would put it—not responding or feeding our energy back to us, we feel frustrated and assume that our ideas and ourselves are rejected.

Active listening is imperative for extroverts to feel supported. Introverts should "turn up the volume" on their listening to demonstrate their active interest in their extrovert peers and subordinates. In other words, they should act a bit like an extrovert—not too much, but a bit.

When a fellow extrovert listens, they nod, they lean forward, they smile or frown—they may not agree wholeheartedly, but they are more fully engaged. As Duffy and Chartrand (2015) describe, extroverts build rapport through explicit active engagement via energy transfer and increased mimicry of the individual to whom they are listening.[5] Surely, introverts have colleagues who act like this, and at times might feel like these colleagues are overdoing it. But we extroverts feed off of the energy of an engaged audience: it is this validation that sparks our energy and allows us to perform at our best. This quality is vital in our organizations, particularly in coherence with the introverted leaders who bring greater thought, analysis and insights.

Please find the following list from *The Introvert Advantage*[6] describing a set of explicit behaviours that demonstrate active listening:

Verbal Listening Cues	Nonverbal Listening Cues
1. Repeat a paraphrased version of the other person's point. 2. Engaging with social cues. Laugh at jokes if appropriate. Be silent if appropriate.	1. Eye contact. 2. Nod and smile. 3. Mirror the posture of the person speaking. 4. Assume an open posture to invite approach and conversation.

Here are a few other ways for introverts to learn to manage extroverts more effectively:

Let Them Be the Centre of Attention on Occasion

This is more natural for extroverts, and not so much for introverts, so let the extroverts be the centre of attention. They are generally good at it, and they will appreciate you letting them do it. They will tend to naturally leave the spirits of the group and get them pumped up to go out and do what they need to accomplish.

Let Them Work the Room With Bigger Groups

We have established that networking is one of the most important strategies for achieving objectives in the corporate world. Extroverts normally maintain well-furnished networks of diverse talent useful for a multitude of scenarios. The introvert can learn from the extrovert in this context. Think of the example of Paul and Hélène Desmarais mentioned below.

Extroverts are more apt to be natural schmoozers, so let them work the room! They genuinely like it, and they tend to do it well.

Canadian billionaire Paul Desmarais II told Karl how he is very much an introvert, and his wife Hélène is a considerable extrovert. How they network is quite different but quite complementary. When they go, as they often do, to a dinner where a few hundred people are ready to sit down to eat at round tables, Paul will sit down one-on-one and have a 30-minute or so chat with another guest and they very much appreciate spending time with one of Canada's top leaders, and Paul spends most of the time asking them questions and being an excellent leader. This is generally very well received by the other person. They are genuinely delighted that one of Canada's most influential business people paid rapt attention to them for half an hour and asked them for their opinion at length. His wife, Hélène, is a very strong extrovert, she goes from group to group working the room, and she spends a bit of time with each group, there is generally laughter and everyone is charmed and pleased that one of Canada's most important people spent time with them, and she speaks to almost every table. Both are very good ways of networking, though quite different in approach. Together, they make a great team.

Encourage Them to Inspire People

With their typical considerable energy, enthusiasm, and pleasure in lifting up the energy in the room, allow them, indeed, encourage them to go out and inspire people; they are generally quite good at this, find joy in doing it, and add considerable leadership value to your organization.

Let Them Take Extrovert Breaks!

I would say extrovert. That being said, the way I recharge my energies is as an introvert. I love my alone time and get exhausted when I spend too much time with people, as much as I like it, so I do need to kind of just take time, put myself out there, shut the noise, and take time with myself, and then with more energy in my body.

O'Nell Agossa (consultant at BCG, a leading global management consulting firm)

Extroverts find time spent away from a dynamic social environment to be tiresome. For an extrovert, it is exhausting to shut up and listen to others for extended periods of time. When this demographic is asked to act introverted for too long, they might become frustrated and desperate to release the energy they have held in before they explode. To prevent such an event from occurring, we must ensure that these social butterflies are given adequate opportunities for extrovert breaks!

Specific suggestions and descriptions of extrovert breaks are listed in the previous chapter. The role of the introverted leader is to watch out for their chatty counterparts and ensure that they, too, are well-equipped with the opportunity and self-determination to assess their own social battery and schedule extroverted breaks as they see fit.

Introverts and the Field of Law

The lawyer archetype is loud, domineering, and extroverted. Surprisingly, in contrast, Eva Wisnik, president of a New York City legal training and placement firm, interviewed 1,600 attorneys over nine years and found that 60% of lawyers she surveyed reported themselves as introverts.[7] Susan Cain, before her authorship of *Quiet*, was also an introverted lawyer and in New York City no less! According to Chloe Sovinee-Dyroff in a 2023 article in the *Georgetown Journal of Legal Ethics*, "the legal profession is rife with extroverts and introverts pretending to be extroverts."[8]

Such a mismatch between the archetypical understanding of a role and those who actually do it is bound to be problematic. Sovinee-Dyroff claims that well-known problems in the industry, including unethical behaviour, the negative public perception of those in the legal profession, and significant career dissatisfaction within the field of law, are in part a consequence of the high value the industry places on extroversion to the exclusion of other traits. From the LSAT's extreme focus on the speed of information processing to the prevalence of the Socratic method in legal classrooms (affectionately known as cold calling and something Gabriele is not looking forward to in her near future), it is clear that the legal education is designed for extroverts to a significant extent. In turn, the legal culture overall places a bias towards competitiveness, homogeneity, and less empathy. In particular, reduced empathy is thematic, as empathy is synonymous with partiality, thus incompatible with impartiality—former President Obama was notably criticized for describing empathy as a skill essential to law for this exact reason. The field of law has "undervalued introverts, to its own detriment."[9]

In addition to the many extroverted tasks that might be required of a lawyer (depending on their practice, of course), such as leading a team to prepare for trial, drawing a hardline during negotiation with the opposite party, presenting a case in court, networking with existing clients, pitching their services to build their clientele base, the role of a lawyer is innately introverted. Long hours must be spent alone reading, writing, and thinking. Further, active listening and creativity in problem-solving are some of many introverted traits critical to a skilled lawyer capable of finding solutions beyond the obvious answers, maybe even developing a strategy nobody has thought of before. Perhaps this career is a truly ambiverted one, drawing upon the toolkits of both introverted and extroverted natures for the ultimate success.

Sovinee-Dyroff argues that since the tendencies of introversion so strikingly oppose the practices that have led to the issues surrounding the legal profession at present, such behaviours are exactly what the doctor has ordered to fix the lawyer. She recommends leaning on the generally higher-than-average moral compasses of introverts to reduce the weaning ethics, promoting collaborative negotiation styles to counter the view of an intimidating and domineering lawyer, and looking to the intrinsic motivation of introverts to promote job satisfaction and reduce burnout.

Further solutions may be found by encouraging authenticity in advocacy style and inclusion of all those who did not fit the traditional lawyer archetype mentioned above—there is a place in the legal field for a wider range of individuals than what it might seem like it currently allows.

For instance, introverts and extroverts will have their own place in the field of law, where their particular set of skills is well-suited to the lawyer tasks they do every day. Extroverts will tend to excel in trial by jury, given their ability to captivate an audience with a story, or maybe with building a clientele base by winning and dining their potential clients and talking big. Introverts, on the other hand, would do really well during a good-faith negotiation, collaborating with the other side to reach a mutually satisfactory arrangement. They would also thrive in the appellate court, which takes place without a big audience and is focused on thorough methodology, detail, and all the technicalities or exceptions rather than the big picture drawn out during a normal trial case. And these are where the ultimate decisions are made.[10]

Our Key Takeaways

#1 Introverts make great leaders, lean into your considerable strengths and make the most of them!

Introverts, we love you and the leadership "experts" have been too negative about you in the past. We apologize. Do take advantage of your strengths outlined in this chapter and other parts of the book, and use them to make your leadership better and improve how management is practiced in the second half of the 2020s.

#2 Lean into the considerable strengths of extroverts and ambiverts and make the most of them!

On the other hand, realize that extroverts and ambiverts have very considerable strengths that complement yours and work as more effective teams to use their strengths combined with yours to improve management and leadership.

#3 Be an ambivert. After all, we are all ambiverts now.

If you are a senior leader or wish to be one. Appreciate and celebrate your strengths as an introvert, but learn to lean into the approaches of extroverts and act like an ambivert from time to time, not all the time, but on occasion, when it would be helpful and make your leadership more effective for the circumstances you are in. But then take an introvert break and return to your normal day-to-day approach.

Notes

1 F1 Desk. "Lewis Hamilton's Dog Roscoe is a Vegan Who Earns $700 per Day." *Crash*, July 3, 2022.
2 Spark, A. and O'Connor, P. "To Get Ahead as an Introvert, Act Like an Extravert. It's Not as Hard as You Think." *The Leadership Quarterly* 32, no. 3 (June 2021): 1001–1009.
3 McChrystal, Stanley, Collins, Tantum, Silverman, David, and Fussell, Chris. *Team of Teams: New Rules of Engagement for a Complex World.* New York: Portfolio/Penguin, 2015.
   And McChrystal, Stanley, Eggers, Jeff, and Mangone, Jason. *Leaders: Myth and Reality.* New York: Portfolio/Penguin, 2018.
4 Khawand, Pierre. "To 'Be' or to 'Be Silent': Taking Mindful Breaks Can Help Introverts Keep Up and Extroverts Flourish in the Workplace." *LinkedIn*, 2018.
5 Duffy, Kathleen A. and Chartrand, Tanya L. "The Extravert Advantage: How and When Extraverts Build Rapport with Other People." *Psychological Science* 26, no. 11 (2015): 1795–1802. https://doi.org/10.1177/0956797615600890.
6 Laney, Marti Olsen. *The Introvert Advantage: How Quiet People Can Thrive in an Extrovert World.* New York: Workman Publishing Company, 2002.

7 Flores, Vanessa A. "Beyond Gregarious: Introverted Attorneys: Surviving in an Extrovert-Driven Society." *Texas Bar Journal* 79, no. 6 (2016): 438–439.
8 Sovinee-Dyroff, Chloe. "Introverted Lawyers: Agents of Change in the Legal Profession." *The Georgetown Journal of Legal Ethics* 25, no. 1 (2023): 118.
9 Sovinee-Dyroff, Chloe. (2023).
10 Lande, John. "Introversion, the Legal Profession, and Dispute Resolution." *University of Missouri Law School Center for the Study of Dispute Resolution*, June 1, 2022.

Chapter 8

What Ambiverts Can Do Better

> I think it's less about working on your [perceived] weaknesses than it is about building up your ability to push yourself outside your comfort zone.
>
> Alisa Cohn (CEO coach from NYC)

Ambiverts are not perfect—they face challenges of their own that they must overcome. During Karl's interviews with executives who self-identified as ambiverts, he learned that these roadblocks may cause hardships equal in difficulty to some of the challenges faced by introverted or extroverted executives.

The nature of the ambivert is so versatile and flexible that it is hard to define, and thus can frustrate people who work for and with you. Someone who so easily adjusts their behaviour to fit given scenarios or other personalities in the room has a novelty persona—one that seems too good to be true. Others involved with ambiverts may misunderstand them, either through a generally false perception of inauthenticity, seemingly excessive flexibility, or confusion and unpredictability surrounding the ambivert's expectations for employees. Ambiverts can be confusing to others, and this is something that an ambivert leader must take considerable care with.

Like their introverted and extroverted counterparts, ambiverts must also take breaks. Switching between introverted and extroverted behaviours may be easier for them, but over time, a large volume of interactions for a high-level executive could still prove tiresome.

Strategies to mitigate both of these potential difficulties for ambiverts are outlined in detail in the following sections.

Avoiding Behaviour That Frustrates People

The ambivert is the best of both worlds. Flexibility between introverted and extroverted behaviours in response to one's surroundings is something like a superpower in the context of internal corporate communication. The ambivert is capable of assuming the strengths of both introverts and extroverts whenever

DOI: 10.4324/9781003612216-9

deemed appropriate. However, such swift and effortless swaps between two communicative styles pose a risk for this corporate superhero. Their capabilities are often misunderstood by their coworkers—this becomes a key weakness for the ambivert, a sort of kryptonite to their effective leadership. If the dynamics of the team break down as a result of this disconnect, the team will not be able to function properly. The following are some strategies to avoid such dangerous misunderstandings.

Open Communication to Cure Unpredictability

Ambiverts may become difficult for subordinates or colleagues to work with, as their actions can be unpredictable and challenging to anticipate. For instance, the unique combination of assertiveness and receptiveness of ambiverted leaders might confuse subordinates on their leader's expectations or approaches to problem-solving. Coworkers often aim to succeed by assessing their leader's preferred communication style and prescribing themselves behaviours compatible with this style. It is more difficult to work with or for someone whose actions you cannot classify into a consistent pattern. The resulting incompatibility will halt productive interactions and fruitful collaboration.

To be honest, there is no exact creative approach or strategy to mitigate a coworker's confusion with your dynamic behaviour. As a leader, keeping your subordinates on their toes might not be the worst outcome. After all, the inability to anticipate their leader's moves will require them to be better prepared for all possible scenarios and think quickly on their feet. The team should expect to develop new skills and excel in compatibility with a multitude of leader personalities as a result of your changing behaviour.

It is important to note that we assume that your dynamic communication style occurs under the guidelines of ambiverted behaviour—as in, the communication style you choose and the decisions you make are rational and consistent with an ambiverted approach to strategic leadership style.

Although unpredictability caused by inconsistency of behaviour should not be an issue on a daily basis, as described previously, there are circumstances in which such confusion can produce substantial drawbacks. There is especially a risk if the unpredictability of communication style diffuses into a general unpredictability surrounding strategic decision-making. Such diffusion can occur if we assume that introverts and extroverts will make different decisions when faced with the same circumstances—a fair assumption to make, in our opinion.

Some cases exist where the stakes are high or there are severe time constraints on a threat or growing problem, and the subordinate is forced to make a quick decision without direct consultation with their superior on how they should address the situation. In times like these, past unpredictable leadership frameworks might lead to confusion regarding decision-making and create uncertainty about how the issue should be addressed in order to maintain team dynamics as the superior would desire. This issue is likely to occur in circumstances where colleagues remain ignorant of the communication strategy behind ambiverted leadership and why certain behaviours are more appropriate in given scenarios.

Again, it is paramount to maintain an open discussion surrounding communication styles in the workplace and ensure that teams can collectively improve both their internal communication with one another and their external communication as a component of corporate strategy. When issues arise, such as the one previously discussed, clarity and assertiveness in communication should help in mitigating any uncertainty of response on behalf of any member of the team.

Help Your Coworkers Learn to Adapt Like You Can

Two of the greatest ambiverted strengths are flexibility and assertiveness. However, ambiverts must always make sure that one does not inhibit the other. While flexibility of approach to match a specific leadership task or team is essential, ambiverts are also at risk of overusing their flexible approach to adapt to corporate structures, routines, or individuals that need to change. Excessive compliance for an ineffective team might hinder productivity instead of promoting it. Over flexibility can create significant issues, such as in cases where the ambivert adapts to an unfavourable or toxic environment to connect with a team when it is clear that assertiveness is what is needed to promote change.

For instance, your team might appreciate your extroverted capabilities, such as public speaking, networking, and taking verbal leadership more than their own. They rely on you to perform this way regularly, as they comprise a group on the introverted side of the spectrum. In the short term, this strategy works well: you have no issue taking the lead during strategy meetings and in public events. However, their heavy reliance on your skills means that they have avoided the development and refinement of their own—their evasion of extroverted behaviours has created an unstable team. If ever faced with a scenario wherein you are unable to contribute, someone ill-prepared to swim will be dropped in the deep end and forced to adapt to extroversion in real time. To put it lightly, this will probably not go smoothly.

A strong and effective ambiverted leader will act as a role model for their team and promote increased practices of ambiversion for everyone. The flexibility of the ambivert does not exist so that the ambivert can micromanage, addressing all of the hardest tasks and making the lives of everyone else on the team easier, but rather to exemplify the benefits of greater flexibility of communication style in the workplace. The ambivert should stick to their guns and remain assertive on the topic of promoting more effective practices within their team. In doing so, each member of the team becomes much better equipped as a valuable working gear of the organization.

Adapting Only to What is Necessary and Being Authentic

> It's more about adaptive leadership style than about thinking you need to re-haul your entire personality.
>
> Alisa Cohn (CEO coach from NYC)

The ambivert is at risk of appearing inauthentic, particularly in circumstances that require a continuous substitution of traits. In these scenarios, a colleague witnessing the expert's transformation between, for example, an attentive and patient listener during an open-hearted conversation about a conflict with a coworker to a smooth jokester proposing a toast to a banquet hall of investors, befriending everyone in a carefree manner may view this swap as effortless—almost too effortless. This colleague may then believe that the ambivert's behaviours are detached and strategic; inauthentic rather than genuine. Authenticity of leadership is all the rage nowadays—so the risk of appearing inauthentic could prove fatal to the support of ambivert leadership.

According to Alisa Cohn, authenticity and ambiversion do not have to be incongruous states:

> Being an ambivert means being aware of your own natural social style, and knowing when the situation may call for just the opposite: The most successful leaders are the ones who can recognise a situation and adapt their style as necessary.

What does authentic leadership look like, and how can we replicate it? Gavin (2019) cites five key behaviours of authentic leaders:

1. They are committed to bettering themselves.
2. They cultivate self-awareness.
3. They are disciplined.
4. They are mission-driven.
5. They inspire faith.[1]

Authentic leadership is dedicated to personal growth, self-awareness, and a genuine quality in their concern for other components of the organization's development.[2]

Mark Shapiro, CEO of the Toronto Blue Jays, believes that authenticity in leadership is synonymous with staying true to oneself despite occupying a powerful position. Shapiro says that,

> The day that I act like a CEO or I act like a President is the day that I lose the authenticity of who I am. So I am very careful every day to act like Mark

Shapiro and I work very hard to be self-aware of who I am, what my values are, and what my identity is.

Consistency is vital for Shapiro to achieve authenticity:

by and large, I think, you know, I'm showing up the same way every day. You know, again, I think, you know, we talked about discipline earlier as being a strength. I think consistency is part of discipline. And I think I'm consistent in the person I am and the leader I am and the way I show up.

Authenticity of leadership is not something you can practice without introspection– it is a trait that comes with passion, dedication, and true belief in both your colleagues and the work that you do. To ensure authenticity to the best of your ability, we recommend assessing your field of work and how it aligns with your beliefs and sense of purpose. Here is where we may take a page from Karl's book on Generation Z (Gen Z) and its emphasis on purpose in the field of work they choose to enter. Purpose is one of the things.[3]

In the 80s and early 90s, the white-collar workers were rather motivated by share price. They would go to considerable lengths to get the share price higher. Thinking back to his time working at IBM, Karl is hard pressed to remember why it was so motivating. Often, their paychecks were central to their lives. Fast forward two decades, and you notice that Gen Z are concerned with a wide range of things. Money is important and they do enjoy making it, however, they long to be part of something bigger than themselves. The workplace is more of a means to an end; it doesn't define them to the degree that it did for too many Boomers. Gen Z are more apt to want to lead a balanced life. They want to be happy at home and happy on the job; money is not as important. A common understanding among Gen Z is that belonging to something bigger than oneself and working towards a goal other than money will result in a more satisfying work-life balance.

Giving your young employees a purpose will enable them to envision a future with your company. Young people are fickle. They are on an endless search for happiness. They want it all and they want it fast. If an organization is unable to map out a road plan, a purpose of employment, they will unfortunately notice a high zero to two years turnover.

Mid-day Squares is the fastest-growing functional chocolate bar on the market. Its trio of founders, Jake Karls, Lezlie Karls Saltarelli, and Nick Saltarelli, are coined "the Tripod" and epitomize Gen Z's outlook on authenticity—raw passion, dedication to their cause, and the courage to present themselves as they are.

Beyond the company's phenomenal sales and passion for its core product, Tripod is committed to a unique digital strategy that presents the true and unfiltered life of entrepreneurship. Lezlie believes that one of the Mid-day Squares' competitive advantages is its capacity for storytelling: in her opinion, "Social media is a forever changing landscape, but storytelling has been around for as long as humans have existed."

The Tripod vows to post utterly authentic, raw content for their viewers in their popular podcast. This unfiltered publication has been highly successful in its aims to portray the behind-the-scenes of building a business—therapy sessions, legal battles, fundraising, and all!

As Gen Z takes over the workforce, corporate movements demanding employee diversity, improved work-life balance, and environmental social governance practices have placed enormous pressure on the traditional chief executive role. After five years of devotion to their company and each other, the Tripod is an unstoppable force. The team is passionate about the products they create, as evidenced by their commitment to maintaining their intersectional positioning in both the chocolate and functional bar markets. Although an uncommon strategy, this podcast certainly portrays the founders' pure authenticity. Perhaps such vulnerability is not for everyone—but it should nonetheless drive the point home about the benefits of staying true to yourself rather than putting on a mask that does not suit you.

Taking Ambivert Breaks

Ambivert breaks are essentially the same concept as we have discussed for introverts and extroverts. The difference is that ambiverts might benefit from either—or both—introvert or extrovert breaks. When the ambivert feels undersocialized, they will take an extrovert break to recharge their batteries. Similarly, if feeling undersocilalized with and tired of extroverted practices, the ambivert could take a moment to recharge as an introvert would. Specific examples of extrovert and introvert breaks are listed in Chapters 5 and 6, respectively. In addition to these, ambivert breaks could be any activity done socially or in solitude, so long as it is classified as a break from work. This section will discuss how ambiverts know when best to take these breaks and how to ensure that they are effective.

Plan Ahead

Let's listen to ambivert, Rob Khazzam, General Manager Uber Canada,

> I have areas of my life where I'm extremely extroverted when I'm out with my friends on the weekends when I go for dinner my friends would describe me as an extrovert but on a day to day basis I do feel that that craving of an introvert which is time alone. I do feel the need to leave the office when

I spend time socializing when I go to events where we do PR or interacting with our team after a few hours I feel exhausted and I need time to recharge and I think knowing that as a professional is important so you know I can plan my day accordingly.

For ambiverts, it is all about balance. Too much time alone, and it will be harder for you to get back into the swing of things socially. By planning ahead, you can mitigate the effects of either over- or under-socialization by scheduling the appropriate breaks in your calendar. This strategy is the best one to ensure consistent socialization, which in turn prevents exhaustion of one communication style and promotes overall work performance.

Recognize that a weekend full of socializing will probably leave you feeling burnt out by Monday, and take steps to make sure that you have enough "me time." For example, you can try to reserve Sunday for solitude so that, come Monday morning, you are ready to meet and engage with people. The same applies to a lack of socializing: if you expect a long and gruelling day of absorbing presentations, plan a social lunch or post-work drink to give yourself the time you need to recalibrate for the following day.

Control Your Environment

Introvert and extrovert breaks are most effective if they are executed properly, as they would be done by introverts and extroverts. Because ambiverts are switching on a regular basis between the two forms of behaviours on the go and generally exhibit twice as many potential responses to given circumstances (sometimes simultaneously), they are more likely to feel as though they are juggling personalities and are less likely to take a break with the meaningful intention to stop, breathe, and rest. Most people cannot truly recharge if they are holding work-related thoughts in the back of their minds.

Ambiverts must consciously make efforts to take meaningful breaks. The easiest thing to do to make sure that you are productive in doing so is placing yourself in the proper environment. If you need a break from everyone, you can try shutting your office door or putting on noise-cancelling headphones for 30 minutes. If you haven't spoken with anyone all day, getting coffee or calling a friend on your break can be extremely energizing. As with everything, flexibility is key, but intention is vital.

We recommended the strategy of planning ahead. Along this line of thought, planning a set time to recharge in a specific environment could be a productive method to ensure that you take your mind off of work and actually recharge. Alternatively, you could ensure that you have a space readily available in your office that allows you to recharge whenever necessary.

Catherine Dagenais, the CEO of SAQ, the liquor store chain which is operated by the Government of Québec, with over 7,000 employees, is an introverted extrovert who recharges by doing both. She says,

> I like to take care of myself so I train I do yoga twice a week and I do, I have an electrical in my office. So when I'm not doing yoga I do the elliptical. So I like to train, I love to walk as well.

By blocking off designated time for a yoga class and keeping the elliptical in her office, Dagenais ensures that she can always take the introvert break she needs. These breaks allow her to reset her mind so that it is fresh and ready to deal with the tasks she faces in the office. If you often forget to take these necessary pauses from rigorous work, we recommend blocking off time in your schedule and holding yourself accountable to sticking to them.

Managing the Mental Toll

It's easy to be swept into obligations that you shouldn't take on if you are in an extroverted mood. If you overcommit, you will start to feel burnt out or anxious, which will become apparent in your work. In a corporate world that is becoming increasingly concerned with openness, communication and group efforts, it is crucial that you take the time to reflect individually. By learning to say no, you are recognizing your need for quiet time and allowing yourself to be a better worker overall.

One of the biggest traps ambiverts fall into is assuming that they cannot get burnt out. In fact, if they aren't careful, ambiverts get burnt out twice as quickly. The key to leading a healthy life is balance, and this area is no exception. The downsides of too much socialization include crabbiness, stress, and strained relationships. On the flip side, spending too much time by yourself can lead to feeling isolated, demotivated, and lonely. Either side can have serious ramifications in both your personal and professional lives. It is all too easy to just keep feeding either your extroverted or introverted side while ignoring the other. There have been many times when ambiverts have felt surprised by the sense of relief she felt after a quick ten-minute conversation, yet experienced the same good feeling when listening to her silent house after returning from a party.

Notes

1 Gavin, Matt. "Authentic Leadership: What It is and Why It's Important." *Harvard Business School Online Business Insights Blog*, December 10, 2019. https://online.hbs.edu/blog/post/authentic-leadership.
2 Perkins, K. M. "Authenticity: The Key to Great Leadership and How to Embrace It." *Forbes*, May 30, 2023. https://www.forbes.com/sites/kmperkins/2023/05/30/authenticity-key-to-great-leadership.
3 Moore, Karl. *Generation Why: How Boomers Can Lead and Learn from Millennials and Gen Z.* Montreal: McGill-Queen's University Press, 2023.

Chapter 9

Striking the Balance as a Junior Employee

Much of the practical advice we have provided thus far was directed towards senior leaders in organizations. It is important, however, to give our next generation of leaders some thoughts as well.

> If I had to give one piece of advice to young professionals who have to navigate today's dynamic globalization, it would be this: there's nothing more important than adaptability. It's the skill to develop. The world has never changed as fast as it is changing today. We need to remain as open-minded and attentive as possible to technical, technological, and social transformations in order to accept and adapt to these changes.
>
> Faisal Kazi (President and CEO at Siemens Canada, an executive with considerable global experience)

As a university professor, Karl has the benefit of having taught over 8,000 of the smartest students in the world at Oxford, Cambridge, and McGill Universities, many of whom have gone on to work for world-class corporations. He takes these lessons directly from these students and provides them to you in this chapter.

As a junior employee (under 30 or so), it is very helpful to understand if you yourself are an introvert, ambivert or extrovert. If you are (or aim to be) on the path to rising the corporate ladder, you may well have to learn to stretch a bit and act like an ambivert. At a younger age, it is prime time for you to work on this skill; you are allowed a bit more latitude to experiment, your habits are less cemented by time, and the burdens of delivering results and being a strong leader are generally considerably less when the stakes are not all on you.

So, we encourage you to try out the introvert or extrovert side of yourself as we discussed in earlier chapters and to experiment so that you can become more comfortable with some variety to your approach. As we age, we often move a little bit towards the centre of the bell curve, as we gain experience and realize that flexibility and awareness are key features of leadership. Please try to hasten that process. In the 20s and into the 30s, many are experimenting with their

DOI: 10.4324/9781003612216-10

leadership skills, and also with their personality in work environments. Both these practices are necessary to determine who you are and who you want to be in your role. A central point for many in their 20s is learning about who they are, and what they are good at and exploring their purpose, at least as it stands at that point, it may well evolve. One of the questions Karl has been asking CEOs now for a couple of years is what is your purpose, when did you find it, and has it evolved? When he asks these questions in class, the MBAs do lean forward, because they (mainly in their late 20s) are actively thinking about these very questions. They are pleased to hear that CEOs' purpose has often evolved over time, but often there is at least some connection to their purpose earlier in their work lives.

It is also very helpful to understand where your managers and peers fall on the spectrum. Earlier in this book, we talked about managing yourself. Beyond managing yourself as a person in your 20s and 30s, we will now also focus on managing your introvert/ambiverted/extrovert bosses and peers.

Learn From (and Respect) Your Elders

Our first recommendation would be to try and heed the advice that we have already outlined. No matter how junior you are, in order to rise up the corporate ladder, it is essential to exhibit the behaviours that people expect of senior executives—put more simply, you have to "fake it until you make it." In doing this, you are learning to act as an introvert or extrovert as the occasion requires—that is, acting like an ambivert.

One of the easiest and most effective ways to maximize your learning is to seek out mentors.

Most CEOs have told Karl that they have mainly learned from observing previous CEOs in action—particularly their direct predecessors. This is especially true when someone has been COO before they become CEO. Two cases of this particularly come to mind. The current CEO of the National Bank of Canada, the sixth largest bank in Canada, with about 27,000 employees, the current CEO was the COO and was very much in the running to be the next CEO, Laurent watched his predecessor Luis with considerable care to see how it was "done in the big leagues." As did Mirko Babic of Bell (a telecoms firm of over 50,000 employees), he spent at least a year as the COO and most likely the next CEO, learning from working closely with the then CEO George Cope.

Many corporations operate mentorship programmes and pair up younger employees starting out with more senior executives. Taking the advice of these seasoned corporate types will do you lots of good. They have thousands of lessons you can learn from without the detriment of whichever painful experience it might have cost them in exchange. It is true that not all teachings of high-level executives will prove directly useful in today's tumultuous and rapidly changing world. However, their wisdom nonetheless retains value, as it could shape your mindset to understand better the business environment you face. They have prospered in the environment which formed the basis for the current one. Veterans of an industry are still one of the greatest resources, even if that industry changes every day. Combined with your modern understanding of the trends and threats you might face and your knowledge of deliberate and emergent strategy, you will be well-equipped to conquer any challenge.

If you are an introverted entry-level employee, for example, there will almost certainly be instances in which you will have to engage with clients or deliver presentations. To shine in these kinds of situations, you might want to consider acting in a more extroverted manner. By the same token, there are countless scenarios in which extroverted employees might want to consider being more introverted for their benefit and the benefit of their team.

Managing Upward Through Your Communication Style

One of the most important jobs in Karl's long career has been learning how to manage upward. We often write and talk about managing (we don't call it managing downward of course) those who work for us, but managing upward is perhaps more important or relevant for most of us. Throughout his long career, Karl has always had a boss. Some people want to be entrepreneurs so that they don't have a boss—but many entrepreneurs have told us that their VC, board, banker, and customers are all "the boss."

Here are a couple of quotes from entrepreneurs about being the only boss as an entrepreneur.

Dax Dasilva, CEO of Lightspeed, a 3,000-person global high-tech firm,

Everyone has a boss. From my experience, when you're VC-backed, your key investors can feel like your boss. And when you're a public company CEO, the same is true of the Chairman and your Board. In both cases, if you retain enough ownership or influence, you can retain the final say on key decisions.

Helge Seetzen, CEO at Tandem Launch, scouts, accelerates, and commercializes early-stage technologies from the world's top universities in close partnership with leading corporations. We collaborate with innovative entrepreneurs and technologists to turn these initial ideas into high-quality startup ventures that our partners then lead to international impact. Helge told us that,

'Boss' has two connotations: somebody who tells you what to do versus somebody to whom you are accountable.

For an entrepreneur, the accountability dimension is actually much wider than for a regular corporate manager. As an officer of a startup, you are accountable to a large number of stakeholders including explicit fiduciary responsibility and moral responsibility toward groups like your employees.

On the "telling what to do" side, it is trickier. Technically, nobody can give direct instructions to a CEO. Even the board can only (legally) hire and fire you. But in practice, *lots* of people will tell you what to do because you have a massive cloud of "dotted line" connections to investors, board members, customers, etc. And because the survival of your business often depends on keeping these groups happy, you tend to try to incorporate their advice/wishes. Karl always tells our entrepreneurs that managing up is more important than managing down for leaders. Find one to three good managers and empower them to manage down, then focus on managing up and expanding your company's ecosystem."

To manage upward, there are a few key principles:

Establish Their Communication Style and Keep Communication Flowing

How does your boss like to communicate and be communicated to? Different people like different approaches. We recommend you use the previous lessons to analyze your boss and approach them in a way that best fits their communication style. Leaning into their preferred approach, even if they are not aware of which it is to them, will make them feel that you are consistent and reliable. You know what to expect, you prepare for it, and this will impress them.

Whether they are extroverts or introverts we would argue (to know one's surprise at this point!) is one of the most important ways of thinking about people (though remember when you have a hammer everything is a nail so they them as multidimensional human beings—you may recall we covered this some detail in Chapter 4). Introverts prefer emails so they can think about things before you show up, extroverts, saying, "Hey let's grab a coffee" fits better with how they approach the world. At this point, we don't need to go on about this. Other things might be doing early morning, lunch or later in the day meetings. We recommend that you lean into their preferred approach. Make sure you ask questions so that you can understand what they want in some detail, and don't be afraid to respectfully suggest ideas, they need them! Part of being an excellent listener is to confirm your understanding of what they are suggesting, we are genuinely surprised how often it really helped to get things straight. If they were not aware of the importance of communication style in the workplace, your suggestions to draw attention to it will be an insightful one they will commend. Now, how do you figure out their preferred style? One way is to ask someone who worked for them for a while, or just ask them. Simple, yes, but it tends to work.

Understand What Motivates Your Boss. What is Their Agenda?

What are they trying to accomplish? What are their priorities? Why are these things important?

Just as your boss will appreciate you understanding their preferred communication style, they will also very much welcome your attempts to understand their objectives, priorities, and goals for the team. If you can understand the motivations behind the strategy they set, you will be able to simulate their approach to create similar future strategies. Even more powerful, if you can provide alternative perspectives on this approach to strengthen it, any good boss would graciously accept this valuable feedback.

When Karl was teaching at Oxford, he got to row for his college. Two of his students rowed for the Oxford University rowing team and rowed in "the Boat Race," the famous race on the Thames River where Oxford and Cambridge, a race watched by hundreds of thousands in person and millions more on television. The way a rowing team must all row together in the same direction is a very appropriate metaphor for how strategy works in an organization. The CEO and C-suite executives set the strategy, and it cascades down to the work that everyone does in the organization, or at least, it should. If we all row together in the same direction, we are more apt to achieve our overall strategy. At a more junior level, we would encourage you to understand how your work fits in with your managers and how your managers support their managers, etc., all the way up to the CEO's strategy.

What you want to do is to try to ensure that you are helping your manager in achieving their top three strategically important goals, if you do, you will be a star and a hero to them. And you are more apt to be promoted and given an excellent performance review, the route to the top.

If you are uncertain, do not assume you know what your superior is thinking. Never be afraid to ask questions—working together with them, through their process, allows you insight into how they think, thus providing further opportunity for you to learn the way they do things.

Bring Solutions, Not Problems

Of course, you should and indeed must talk to your boss about problems, this was what Karl taught at IBM years ago, but it is still valid today, not all older ideas are bad. A star young person learns to think about the possible solutions to the problem. The boss chooses which of the options you present, but over time, they will tend to choose the one you recommend. This is a way that managers work with and train young employees to learn to deal with problems on their own and only bring problems to them which are bigger ones with bigger potential impact and where you genuinely want to get their wisdom (and possibly get them on board if the ship starts leading a bit). As you handle more and more problems, you gain confidence and you only take the appropriate ones to them, save them time, and it is a way of teaching/training/coaching you.

No Surprises, Make Them Look Good

Unlike wine or cheese, bad news ages poorly. When you have news, bad or very good, it is better to allow your manager to be aware of it sooner rather than later, that way they can reflect on the best approach to it and perhaps inform their manager. Something bad or very good happening in your area of responsibility is something you do not want your boss or your boss's boss to ask you about, and you were not aware of it, so make sure this doesn't happen to your boss because of you not updating them, you should have.

Reverse Mentor Them

Karl had a book, *Generation Why: How Boomers Can Lead and Learn from Millennials and Gen Z*. One of the best-received ideas from the book was that younger people should reverse mentor their old bosses and colleagues. In that book, Karl argues that the undergrad students who work for him (like Gabby a few years ago now) mentor him 30% of the time, that is, he learns from them how to be more effective in today's, not yesterday's world, with their help, guidance and tutelage. The flip side is that 70% of the time, Karl is mentoring them— it is a two-way street these days. This hearkens back to the idea that generals too often fight the battles of their youth. So, to help older people get with it, you need to reverse mentor them.

This is an idea that might take some getting used to for the older generations, but we see it as your job to do so. Perhaps sharing with them an article on it might be a good starting place. Suggest that they read this book or one of the articles in the footnote at the end of this sentence (introvertish thing) and suggest that it is something to discuss over coffee (extrovertish thing).[1]

Introversion and Extroversion Beyond Communication Style in the Corporate Environment

At its foundation, introversion and extroversion relate to where we get our energy. It is most commonly understood through communication style because of the predominant stereotypes of chatty extroverts and timid introverts that we have mentioned several times throughout this book. We also discuss these concepts primarily through communication style in the corporate world—our advice offers strategies on how to network more effectively, build relationships, rally a crowd, listen better, think more analytically, resolve conflicts, and understand the needs of your boss. Surely, these skills are all essential for a successful career. Our interviews with the various executives, entrepreneurs, or otherwise exceptional individuals demonstrate that at some level, it is necessary to be able to act like an introvert and an extrovert at times.

However, it is also important to recognize that there is much more to introversion and extroversion than simply what it does for you as an employee. The flexibility of your communication style and the awareness as to when certain behaviours best fit the situation around you are tools which will serve you well beyond a corporate career. They are tools which improve your life in general.

Outside the realm of communication, greater flexibility in a person means they excel in versatility and are well-equipped to handle a variety of tasks. Greater awareness of a person's surroundings makes them more capable of understanding all layers of the environment around them, so they are able to make the most well-informed decision since they have obtained a comprehensive understanding of the facts before them. By establishing the necessary flexibility and awareness to successfully switch between both introverted and extroverted behaviours, one develops these attributes such that they become applicable to areas far beyond engaging with your colleagues or listening better.

Since joining Karl's research, Gabriele has noticed her own development of greater flexibility and awareness and its implications on both her communication style and her life, in general.

While she is rather extroverted and gains energy by spending time with others, she has also discovered an appreciation for spending time alone with her thoughts. Gabriele now identifies as an ambivert, as she requires both socialization and internal reflection to recharge her batteries and be her best self.

Regarding awareness, Gabriele has become much more capable of reading a room and knowing when her contributions are valuable, as opposed to when they are not moving a conversation forward and should be omitted. This skill has allowed her to become a better listener, which allows her to understand a situation, ask more effective questions, target the root of problems, and offer solutions or advice if necessary. She can now sense and understand the unspoken preferences of professors, other classmates, work colleagues, and anyone, really.

The most clear example is when Gabriele can perceive some form of undeclared reasoning for a certain objective or behaviour. Perhaps something is not getting done, and someone is unreasonably frustrated in consideration of what has been explicitly stated as desired. This could easily cause conflict because it constitutes an overreaction. The best way to address this issue, Gabriele has found, is by sensing that there exists some concern or reasoning and directly addressing this with the other person. Oftentimes, the ulterior reasoning may be inferred from one's surroundings. The other person is usually grateful you were aware enough to sense an underlying issue and kind enough to attempt to resolve it. People are often surprised and impressed at the insights one might gain from a more keen awareness of one's surroundings; all it takes, really, is to pay attention to what is going on.

Beyond school and work environments, these skills have made her a better friend to others and a better person in general. Not only is she more aware of those around her and how to best serve their needs, but also how to manage her own energy capacity and when she needs to take a break. She now knows when she has spent too long in one environment, either an excessively social or isolating one, and that she must switch out of it before she gets in a mood.

Gabriele's flexibility in communication style also makes her a more interesting person. Since she can now adjust her energy output based on the needs of those around her, she has been able to expand her network to include extreme extroverts, extreme introverts, and all those in between. She also enjoys a variety of activities with these different types of friends, which makes her more adaptable and easy-going. She, herself, benefits from the unique experiences she would not have agreed to partake in prior to this personal development.

Note

1 Management consulting giant, Oliver Wyman published article in 2023 interviewing Karl about this idea, you can access it at Oliver Wyman Forum. "Leaders Need to Inspire Young Workers to Retain Them: Interview with Karl Moore." *Oliver Wyman Forum*, June 2023. https://www.oliverwymanforum.com/gen-z/2023/jun/leaders-need-to-inspire-young-workers-to-retain-them.html.and there is also an article of Karl's, *cf.* Moore, Karl. "The Virtues of Youth." *Dialogue Journal* (September 2023). Duke University. https://www.dukece.com/insights/the-virtues-of-youth/.

Chapter 10

Conclusion

That's it, we are bringing it to a close. Hopefully, this book has helped you better understand introverts, ambiverts and extroverts as leaders. More fundamentally, it has helped you to better understand yourself and consider how you might manage yourself, manage and work with others, and manage upward as a leader. And also at home to be a better partner and parent. Extraversion, introversion are only one of the Big Five personality characteristics, human beings are wonderfully complex. But we believe and research supports that it is most likely the most important.

A famous saying states, "If you have a hammer, everything is a nail." Being an introvert, ambivert, or extrovert is only one dimension of being a human being; there are many others that impact how we lead and live. However, we believe and argue in this book that it is an important one. One that you should consider, reflect on, and modify your behaviour a bit in order to be a more effective leader, follower, partner, parent, etc.

The key message of this book is that, while we are all born with predisposed strengths and weaknesses, many of which are attributed to where we fall on the introversion-extroversion spectrum, we are not bound more than a bit by our natural "hardwiring."

In the book's first half, we argued that it is not only possible for introverts, extroverts, and ambiverts to overcome their weaknesses, but that, to rise up the corporate ladder, it is essential. And not just to focus on where we fall short to also capitalize on the considerable and valuable strengths of all three. To a considerable degree, this book is based on research, the existing literature, but also the hundreds of interviews done with senior executives for this book. It is grounded in the reality of leading in today's world. A more turbulent world than in years in more recent living memory. There is less certainty, and to appropriately deal with it, in most cases, the solution is to listen more to people who are dealing with that changing world on a day-to-day basis, that is, your front line troops, who are often younger than the people at the top. The people at the top are held, rightly so, responsible for if our strategy succeeds or fails. But in most cases in today's world, they should, must, listen more, be less hierarchical than

DOI: 10.4324/9781003612216-11

in the past. This more introverted approach is what the world, by and large, is calling for.

On the other hand, in a hard, challenging world, we also need the energy, positive vibes, and the bigger personalities of the extrovert. We need inspiring leadership. This may not come naturally, but c'est la vie, what many of us must learn to do.

In the latter half, we focused on providing the reader with practical suggestions on how they can act on our recommendations. Our hope is that this book will bring the best out of every introvert, extrovert, and ambivert that reads it.

Love to hear your stories, please contact Karl at karl.moore@mcgill.ca and share with Gabby and him your real stories so we can continue to learn about his fascinating part of human behaviour!

Suggestions for Further Reading

Books and Articles We Recommend

Cain, Susan. *Quiet, The Power of Introverts in a World That Can't Stop Talking.* Crown Publishers, New York City, U.S.A., 2013.

Cain, Susan. *Quiet Power: The Secret Strengths of Introverted Kids.* Puffin Books, London, U.K., 2017.

Dennis, Alexander, Barlow, Jordan and Dennis, Alan. The Power of Introverts: Personality and Intelligence in Virtual Teams. *Journal of Information Management Systems,* 39:1, 102–129, April 2022.

Emre, Merve. *The Personality Brokers: The Strange History of Myers-Briggs and the Birth of Personality Testing.* Doubleday, New York City, U.S.A., 2018.

Farrell, Maggie. Leadership Reflections: Extrovert and Introvert Leaders. *Journal of Library Administration,* 57:4, 436–443, 2017.

Freyd, M. Introverts and Extroverts. *Psychological Review,* 31:1, 74–87, 1924.

Grant, Adam, Francesca, Gino and Hofmann, David. Reversing the Extraverted Leadership Advantage: The Role of Employee Proactivity. *Academy of Management Journal,* 54, 528–550, 2011.

Kuijpers, Evy, Joerie, Hofmans and Bar, Wille. Stop Telling Introverts to Act Like Extroverts. *Harvard Business Review,* October, 2022.

Laney, Marti Olsen. *The Introvert Advantage: How Quiet People Can Thrive in an Extrovert World.* Workman Publishing Company, New York City, U.S.A., 2002.

Nelson, Sarah. *How To Parent An Introvert: Recognize What Works, Embrace the Quiet and Support Your Introvert.* Seaview Publishing Ltd., Australia, 2024.

Pollard, Lewis and Lewis, Derek. *The Introvert's Edge to Networking: Work the Room. Leverage Social Media. Develop Powerful Connections.* HarperCollins Leadership, New York, 2024.

Pollard, Matthew and Lewis, Derek. *The Introvert's Edge: How the Quiet and Shy Can Outsell Anyone.* Amazon, New York City, U.S.A., 2018.

Wilding, Melody. An Introvert's Guide to Visibility in the Workplace. *Harvard Business Review,* March 2024.

Our Research in the Media and Our Publications

3 Ways to Be a More Effective Ambivert, Karl Moore and Sara Avramovic, *Quiet Revolution,* September 2023.

5 Tips to Take the Anxiety Out of Networking From A VP of Growth, *Forbes.com,* Karl's blog, July 26, 2023.

A legjobb vezetők személyiségjegyei, *Novekedes*, April 9, 2021.

Combining Introverts and Extroverts, Bartley, *The Economist*, March 18, 2021.

Csak a nagyarcú nagydumásokból lesznek sikeres vezetők? Tévedés.

Extrovert or Introvert? Think Again. The Pandemic Probably Made You Something in Between. By *Rebecca Knight*, August 11, 2021, *Business Insider*. Also came out in Spanish and German.

Ha Mesmo Uma Personalidade Talhada Para Vencer, *Visao*, April 4, 2021.

How To Be Everyone's Type, Kerry Potter, *The Mail on Sunday*, April 30, 2022.

How To Network Like an Introvert, Karl Moore, *Quiet Revolution*, March 2023.

Introvert, Extort or Other? Welcome to the Age of the Ambivert, *The Guardian*, Emma Beddington, December 2, 2021.

Kit rejt az ambiverált személyiségtípus?, *Noklapja*, October 29, 2021.

Kopplingen Mellan Personlighet Och Framgang, Oscar Jangnemyr, *Dagens PS*, March 27, 2012.

Ky është lloji më i mirë i personalitetit për sukses, March 23, 2021, Nga Bryan Lufkin, *ABC News*, 24/7.

Le Lien Entre personnalite et resussite, *Le Nouvel Economist*, March, 2012.

Molnár Balázs, *Haszon*, April 02, 2021.

Moore, Karl. Ambivert Leaders Are More Effective. *Duke University Management Development Strategy*, October 3, 2023.

Moore, Karl. Five Types of Extrovert Breaks. *Wharton Leadership Digest*, Summer 2019.

Moore, Karl. Why Leaders Should Channel Their Inner Introverts. *Wharton Leadership Digest*, Summer 2015.

Moore, Karl, Garcia, Kat and Labrosse, Marie. How Can Introverts and Extroverts Work in Isolation. *Wharton Leadership Digest*, April–May 2020.

Moore, Karl and Liu, Willing. Can Introverts Survive in "Extroverted Careers?" *Harvard Business Review*, January 2021.

Not an Introvert or An Extrovert? 8 Signs You Could Be an Ambivert, Linda Rogers, *Reader's Digest Australia*, March 2021.

The Atlantic, Fear of an Awkward President, August 22, 2023, quotes our *Harvard Business Review* article.

The Link Between Personality and Success, The Bartleby Column, *The Economist*, March 20, 2021.

The Quiet Side Of F1-Introverted Qualities Of Lauda, Stroll & Hamilton, *Forbes.com*, June 7, 2024, Karl's blog.

To Each Their Own: Giving Feedback to Introverts and Extroverts, Karl Moore, *Quiet Revolution*, February 2022.

Wedding Advice for the Quiet Brides in Your Life, Adrienne Jung and Karl Moore, *Quiet Revolution*, April 2023.

Who Does Best at Work: Extroverts or Introverts?, *The Australian* March 27, 2021.

Why Ambiverts Are Better Leaders, *BBC World*, March 22, 2021.

Zašto su ambiverti bolje vođe? *Dalmatinski*, March 26, 2021.

About the Authors

Gabriele graduated with distinction from McGill University's Desautels, where she joined the book team as a contributor. Gabriele also had the role of producer of Karl's CEO radio show, publishing over 100 episodes based on Karl's interviews with industry leaders. She has worked with Karl to occasionally contribute articles to his weekly *Forbes* column. Upon her graduation from McGill, Gabriele deferred her acceptance to Osgoode Hall Law School for one year to accept the invitation from Karl to coauthor *We Are All Ambiverts Now*. She now attends Osgoode Hall Law School as a first-year student, where she has joined the *Osgoode Hall Law Journal* as Senior Editor.

Gabriele Hartshorne-Mehl
Alumna, Desautels Faculty of Management, McGill University;
JD Candidate, Osgoode Hall Law School, York University

Prior to his academic career, Dr. Moore worked for a decade for IBM/Hitachi. Before McGill, he taught at Oxford University for five years, he was the founding strategy teacher on the Oxford MBA at the Said Business School back in the late 1990s. He has published 28 refereed journal articles; this is his 11th book.

He has presented/taught his research at Stanford, Harvard Business School, Darden, Duke, Oxford, IIM Bangalore, Renmin University (Beijing), Reykjavik University, and IMD. His research on ambiverts has been highlighted in *The Economist, The Financial Times, The Globe and Mail, the New York Times, the BBC*, and other media around the world.

Karl hosts a weekly national radio programme, "The CEO Series" on Bell Media network across Canada. It is an hour-long one-on-one with a CEO or other senior leader which he has done for over a dozen years. This show, along with his CEO Insights class for McGill MBAs, where they have 33 CEOs a year, has allowed Karl to interview over 1,000 CEOs. One of the few advantages of being older is that older people have done things longer, far longer, than most. His tenth book, *Generation Why: How Boomers and Xers Can Lead and Learn from Millennials and Gen Z* came out in 2023.

Karl Moore
Associate Professor, McGill University

Appreciation

A crowd of people helped create this book. For six years the Desautels Faculty of Management at McGill provided Karl with three or four very bright undergraduate students to help with the research for this book, many were part of the Integrated Management Student Fellowship (IMSF) programme run by Alexandra Eva Samra and Dr. Sabine K. Dhir of the Desautels Faculty of Management at McGill University. The IMSF is an experiential leadership development opportunity offered through the BCom programme designed for undergraduate students seeking to create real-world impact, in the case of this book, we really believe they accomplished that if readers learn from our work, and on occasion, act a bit differently.

In 2024: Zach Gallant, Talia Jaoude, Hanna Sproat, and Jules Vuillemin were our most recent team.

In 2023: Four more stars: Ali Eissa, Hanna Goh, Xuefei Ren, and Esteban Ronsin.

In 2022: Gabriele Hartshorne-Mehl—the coauthor! Bo Wen Chen, who also organized our annual Hot Cities of the World Tour to Ghana and the Ivory Coast, and the inestimable Carl Johan Leander.

Way back in 2021, Tom Berger and Khaled Khadam. A particular standout was Xuefei Ren—thanks so much!

But we must very much thank and acknowledge the executives we interviewed who provide the heart of this book, many are quoted in this book, and without you, it would not been as insightful as we hope it is.

And of course, Susan Cain. Back in 2012, Karl wrote a piece for *Forbes.com* entitled, "Introverts No Longer the Quiet Followers of Extroverts" based on Susan's bestseller, *Quiet*. Karl wrote it with Emma Bambrick, a student of his at the time. Emma helped organize one of our annual Hot Cities of the World Tour to Russia. Before university, she was an actress in the television show Degrassi High. The day they put their post out, it got over 66,000 views, five hundred times better than the average piece Karl did for *Forbes*. They were thrilled, but it also indicated the high interest levels in the topic, which effectively helped inspire this book.

Karl went down to Quiet House outside New York City twice to interview Susan for his national radio show, the CEO Series, and had some long talks with her and wrote a few pieces for her *Quiet Revolution*. Susan has been an inspiration!

Other people include Belgium friend and colleague Eden Elliot Locoge. McGill students Xuefei Sophie Ren, Kyra Odell, Katherine Lake, Morielle Daisy Rubineau, Reza Rehman, and star McGill alumni Fiona Buell, we apologize if we have missed anyone!

We would also like to thank the clergy who sat down with Karl: Roger Labelle, Lorenzo DellaForesta, Ken Gordon, Gary Moore, Rabbi Lisa Grushcow, Skúli S. Ólafsson, and Bill Hall.

And for intellectual stimulation, friendship, and mentoring Henry Mintzberg and Dick Pound.

Index

For Product Safety Concerns and Information please contact our EU
representative GPSR@taylorandfrancis.com
Taylor & Francis Verlag GmbH, Kaufingerstraße 24, 80331 München, Germany